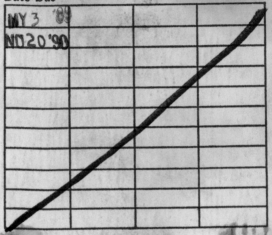

THE PROCESS OF EDUCATION

The Process of Education

JEROME S. BRUNER

HARVARD UNIVERSITY PRESS · CAMBRIDGE

Distributed in Great Britain by
Oxford University Press, London

Library of Congress Catalog Card Number 60-15235
Printed in the United States of America

FOR

JANE, ANGUS, BONNIE, WHIT, LYN, SANDY,
AND JOCK

MEMBERS OF THE WOODS HOLE CONFERENCE

Dr. Carl Allendoerfer	University of Washington	Mathematics
Dr. Richard Alpert	Harvard University	Psychology
Dr. Edward Begle	Yale University	Mathematics
Dr. John Blum	Yale University	History
Dr. Jerome S. Bruner, Director	Harvard University	Psychology
Dr. C. Ray Carpenter	Pennsylvania State University	Psychology
Dr. John B. Carroll	Harvard University	Education
Dr. Henry Chauncey	Educational Testing Service	Education
Mr. Donald Cole	Phillips Exeter Academy	History
Dr. Lee Cronbach	University of Illinois	Psychology
Mr. Gilbert Finlay	University of Illinois	Physics
Dr. John H. Fischer	Teacher's College, Columbia University	Education
Mr. John Flory	Eastman Kodak Company	Cinematography
Dr. Francis L. Friedman	Massachusetts Institute of Technology	Physics
Dr. Robert M. Gagne	Princeton University	Psychology
Dr. Ralph Gerard	University of Michigan	Biology
Dr. H. Bentley Glass	Johns Hopkins University	Biology
Dr. Arnold Grobman	American Institute of Biological Sciences	Biology
Dr. Thomas S. Hall	Washington University	Biology
Dr. Bärbel Inhelder	Institut Rousseau, Geneva	Psychology
Dr. John F. Latimer	George Washington University	Classics
Dr. George A. Miller	Harvard University	Psychology
Dr. Robert S. Morison	Rockefeller Foundation	Medicine
Dr. David L. Page	University of Illinois	Mathematics
Mr. Richard Pieters	Phillips Academy, Andover	Mathematics
Dr. Wm. C. H. Prentice	Swarthmore College	Psychology
Dr. Paul C. Rosenbloom	University of Minnesota	Mathematics
Dr. Kenneth W. Spence	State University of Iowa	Psychology
Dr. H. Burr Steinbach	University of Chicago	Biology
Dr. Donald Taylor	Yale University	Psychology
Dr. Herbert E. Vaughan	University of Illinois	Mathematics
Dr. Randall M. Whaley	Purdue University	Physics
Dr. Don Williams	University of Kansas City	Cinematography
Dr. Jerrold Zacharias	Massachusetts Institute of Technology	Physics

PREFACE

In September 1959 there gathered at Woods Hole on Cape Cod some thirty-five scientists, scholars, and educators to discuss how education in science might be improved in our primary and secondary schools. The ten-day meeting had been called by the National Academy of Sciences, which, through its Education Committee, had been examining for several years the long-range problem of improving the dissemination of scientific knowledge in America. The intention was not to institute a crash program, but rather to examine the fundamental processes involved in imparting to young students a sense of the substance and method of science. Nor was the objective to recruit able young Americans to scientific careers, desirable though such an outcome might be. Rather, what had prompted the meeting was a conviction that we were at the beginning of a period of new progress in, and concern for, creating curricula and ways of teaching science, and that a general appraisal of this progress and concern was in order, so as to better guide developments in the future.

Major efforts in curriculum design had been launched by leading physicists, mathematicians, biologists, and chemists, and similar projects were in prospect in other fields of scientific endeavor. Something new was stirring in the land. A tour of the United States in the summer of 1959 would have revealed a concentration of distinguished mathematicians in Boulder, Colorado, engaged in writing new textbooks for primary, junior high, and high school grades. In Kansas City, there could be found a group of first-class biologists busily producing films on subjects such as the structure of the cell and photosynthesis for use in tenth-grade biology courses. In Urbana, Illinois, there was a flurry of work on the teaching of fundamental mathematical concepts to gradeschool children, and in Palo Alto one might have found a mathematical logician at work trying out materials for teaching geometry to children in the beginning grades of school. In Cambridge, Massachusetts, work was progressing on an "ideal" physics course for high school students, engaging the efforts not only of text writers and film producers but also of men who had earned world renown in theoretical and experimental physics. At various centers throughout the country, teachers were being trained to teach this new physics course by others who had already tried it. Preliminary work was under way in Boulder on a junior high school course in biology, and a group of chemists were similarly engaged in their field in Portland, Oregon. Various learned societies were searching for and finding ways of establishing contact between their leading scholars and educators in the schools. For their part, educators and psychologists were examining anew the nature of teaching methods and curricula and were becoming increasingly ready to examine fresh approaches. The time was indeed ripe for an over-all appraisal of the situation.

Various organizations charged with one or another responsibility in the field of scientific education and research had also reached a point at which a general examination of progress and prospects was in order. The National Academy of Sciences had engaged in considerable discussion about the manner in which it might facilitate a closer relation between scientists in universities and those charged with teaching in schools, as had the American Association for the Advancement of Science and the Carnegie Corporation of New York. These organizations were generous in their counsel during the planning of the Conference. The National Science Foundation had, so to speak, already gone into business: it was principally through its financial aid and moral support that various of the curriculum projects mentioned above had got under way. It also provided financial support for the Woods Hole Conference, as did the United States Office of Education, the Air Force, and the RAND Corporation.

The Conference, whose members are listed at the head of the book, was unique in composition. Virtually all of the curriculum projects mentioned earlier were represented by scientists who had been engaged in the process of writing texts, teaching the new courses, or preparing films or other materials. In addition, there were psychologists who had devoted a major part of their research lives to the examination of intelligence, learning, remembering, thinking, and motivation. Strange as it may seem, this was the first time psychologists had been brought together with leading scientists to discuss the problems involved in teaching their various disciplines. The psychologists themselves represented a wide spectrum of points of view—behavioristic, Gestalt, psychometric, the developmental viewpoint of the Geneva school, and the rest.

The differences, however, paled before the issues that were to be faced. The group was leavened by a representation of professional educators—teachers, deans, experts in audio-visual methods. Two of the Conference members, finally, were historians. It had been our conviction in planning the Conference that it would be unwise to limit ourselves exclusively to the teaching of science, that the eventual problem would be more general than that, and that it would be in the interest of perspective to compare the issues involved in teaching science with those in a more humanistic field, such as history. The conviction turned out to be a sound one, and our historians contributed mightily to the proceedings.

The conduct of the Conference at Woods Hole will help explain the existence of this book. The opening days were given over to a round-the-clock series of progress reports and appraisals of the work of various curriculum projects—the School Mathematics Study Group, the University of Illinois Committee on School Mathematics, the University of Illinois Arithmetic Project, the Minnesota School Mathematics Center, the Biological Sciences Curriculum Study, and the Physical Science Study Committee. In addition, there were searching reports on requirements for a curriculum in American history. We also took time to examine some recent research related to the educational effort. Demonstration films were shown by Dr. Richard Suchman on the Illinois Studies in Inquiry Training, dealing with how children may be educated to the formulation of searching questions, and also by Dr. Bärbel Inhelder on the recent work of the Geneva group on the thought processes of young children. Indeed, lest the Conference get too remote from the direct problems of teaching, an afternoon was given over to a class demonstration of the techniques used by the Illinois Arithmetic Project, with Dr. David Page, its director, serving as teacher. Teaching machines were demonstrated by Professor B. F. Skinner of Harvard, and the demonstration led to a lively, at times stormy, discussion. Late in those opening evenings, one could relax to instructional films in biology and physics. Time was well filled.

A few days after the Conference opened, its members were divided into five work groups—one concerned with the "Sequence of a Curriculum," a second with "The Apparatus of Teaching," a third with "The Motivation of Learning," a fourth with "The Role of Intuition in Learning and Thinking," and a fifth with "Cognitive Processes in Learning." * The second half of the Conference was devoted almost wholly to the activities of these work groups. Each prepared a lengthy report, and as these were being readied, they were presented to the Conference for debate. While there was considerable

* The members of the various work groups were as follows: "Sequence of a Curriculum," John Blum, Gilbert Finlay, Arnold Grobman, Robert S. Morison, William C. H. Prentice, Herbert E. Vaughan; "The Apparatus of Teaching," C. Ray Carpenter, John B. Carroll, John H. Fischer, John Flory, H. Bentley Glass, Donald Taylor, Don Williams; "The Motivation of Learning," Richard Alpert, Lee J. Cronbach, John F. Latimer, Richard Pieters, Paul C. Rosenbloom, Kenneth W. Spence; "The Role of Intuition in Learning and Thinking," Henry Chauncey, Robert M. Gagne, Ralph Gerard, George A. Miller, Jerrold Zacharias; "Cognitive Processes in Learning," Edward G. Begle, Jerome S. Bruner, Donald Cole, Francis L. Friedman, Bärbel Inhelder, David L. Page, H. Burr Steinbach. An Executive Committee served to coordinate the work of the Conference. It consisted of Edward G. Begle, John Blum, Henry Chauncey, Lee J. Cronbach, Francis L. Friedman, Arnold Grobman, Randall M. Whaley, and Jerome S. Bruner, *Chairman*.

agreement in the various work groups on major emphases, plenary sessions of the Conference were more concerned with debating the issues, and no effort was made to reach a consensus of the Conference as a whole. And herein lies the origin of the present book.

The reports of the various work groups, copies of which can be obtained through the National Academy of Sciences in Washington, were obviously prepared under pressure and with a view to debate. They were not designed to be definitive statements or manifestoes. Yet there were certain recurrent themes that emerged in these reports and at the Conference generally, and it would have been unfortunate indeed to lose these in the maze of compromise wherein thirty-five spirited men reach agreement on what should constitute a final report.

It fell to the Chairman, then, to prepare a Chairman's Report—perforce a selective account of what in his view were the major themes, the principal conjectures, and the most striking tentative conclusions reached. In a proper sense it is the Chairman who is principally responsible for the pages that follow, however much he made every effort to reflect the thought of his colleagues. In drafting the present document, consequently, I have made liberal use of the papers prepared by the work groups and of notes taken at the plenary sessions. In preparing a first draft of the Report for circulation, I leaned particularly upon two members of the Conference, Professor Francis Friedman of M.I.T. and Dr. Richard Alpert of Harvard, who helped not only in the preparation of outlines but also in drafting some of the ideas contained in the outlines. When a first draft of the Chairman's Report was completed, copies of it were sent to all of the members of the Conference for comment and criticism. Several colleagues wrote long commentaries; virtually all had their say in the margins. There were amplifications, dissents here and there, expressions of affirmation, urgings to more extreme statements or cautions against them, a few complaints about ideas omitted and some about ones that had been included or added in the spirit of retrospect. One extended comment pressed the point that the views of Piaget concerning the transition from preoperational to operational thought had been given too prominent a place in the Report. Another complained that the first draft had given short shrift to the problem of teaching aids and had neglected the views of our audio-visual professionals who had urged a "balanced system of teaching aids" consisting of well-tested devices. In the end, the section on aids was expanded, although the doctrine of the "balanced system" was subordinated to what appeared to me to be the prevailing view of the discussions: that aids are instruments to help attain an educational objective, and that it is these objectives and not the existence of apparatus that determine balance.

In short, the preparation of a final draft was greatly aided by the comments of participants—though again it was not undertaken in the spirit of trying to find a consensus. Rather, the pages that follow constitute my conception of the "sense of the meeting" and inevitably will reflect the biases and predilections I bring to the task. At the same time, this book represents a set of views that grew out of the Conference and intense correspondence that followed it.

In preparing the final draft, in the winter following

the Conference, I benefited particularly from several helpful discussions with Woods Hole colleagues. Perhaps the most thorough going-over of the final draft took place in Urbana, Illinois, where Lee Cronbach, Gilbert Finlay, and David Page joined me in what amounted to an intensive seminar on points that had remained moot after the months of correspondence and exchanging of drafts. In Cambridge, I also had the benefit of continuing discussion with my colleagues Richard Alpert and George Miller of Harvard, and Francis Friedman and Jerrold Zacharias of M.I.T. Two men closely associated with primary and secondary education who were not at Woods Hole, Mr. Paul Brandwein and Mr. Edward Yeomans, have also read and commented on the manuscript.

In a cooperative enterprise such as this, there are many people who come to deserve special gratitude. Foremost among these is the man who not only had the idea of calling the Conference, but who implemented it in all possible ways by his intelligent and devoted labors. Dr. Randall Whaley, Director of the Education Office in the National Academy of Sciences, had the idea, arranged for the financing of the Conference and for its housing, helped recruit its members, and generally served to keep the proceedings moving effectively. Dr. Whaley was on leave to the National Academy from Purdue University, where he has now returned as Associate Dean of Sciences. The work of the Conference itself was enormously facilitated by the hard and subtle labors of a staff consisting of Mrs. Eleanor Horan of Harvard University, Mrs. Elizabeth Ramsey of the National Academy of Sciences,

Miss Mildred Runciman of the Rockefeller Foundation, and Miss Margaret Gazan of M.I.T. Mr. Robert Green of the National Academy expedited countless details ranging from having cars meet men who arrived on airplanes in the weather-bedeviled schedules of Cape Cod to obtaining the cooperation of children for demonstrations of the teaching of arithmetic. Finally, it would be difficult to express sufficient thanks to the many kind offices done us by Rear Admiral B. van Mater, U.S.N. (ret.), and his staff at Woods Hole. We were housed in the summer headquarters of the National Academy there, with Admiral van Mater as a most effective chief administrative officer.

I should like also to express my thanks to Harvard University for handling many financial details of the Conference on behalf of the National Academy and particularly to the Director of the Harvard Office for Research Contracts, Mr. Richard Pratt, who combines administrative acumen and a sense of humor to an extraordinary degree.

Many of the ideas that emerged at the Conference and after have long and honorable lineages in the history of educational thought. I, as Chairman of the Conference and author of this Report, apologize for the virtual absence of bibliographical citation in the pages that follow. Our thinking has been shaped and aided, obviously, by the literature related to this subject—and it is a vast literature. In writing this book, I have not sought to do justice to the parentage of ideas, a task more properly undertaken by a more scholarly volume. One such volume, containing a wisely assembled collection of readings, is Professor Robert Ulich's *Three Thousand Years of Educational Wisdom* (Cambridge, Massachusetts, 1959).

Thanks are due, finally, to Harvard University Press for thoughtful and swift publishing.

Jerome S. Bruner

Cambridge, Massachusetts
May 1960

CONTENTS

THE PROCESS OF EDUCATION

1

INTRODUCTION

EACH generation gives new form to the aspirations that shape education in its time. What may be emerging as a mark of our own generation is a widespread renewal of concern for the quality and intellectual aims of education—but without abandonment of the ideal that education should serve as a means of training well-balanced citizens for a democracy. Rather, we have reached a level of public education in America where a considerable portion of our population has become interested in a question that until recently was the concern of specialists: "What shall we teach and to what end?" The new spirit perhaps reflects the profound scientific revolution of our times as well. The trend is accentuated by what is almost certain to be a long-range crisis in national security, a crisis whose resolution will depend upon a well-educated citizenry.

One of the places in which this renewal of concern has expressed itself is in curriculum planning for the elementary and secondary schools. Several striking developments have taken place. There has been an unprecedented participation in curriculum development by university scholars and scientists, men distinguished for their work at the frontiers of their respective disciplines. They have been preparing courses of study for elementary and secondary schools not only reflecting recent advances in science and scholarship but also embodying bold ideas about the nature of school experience. Perhaps the most highly developed curriculum of this kind is the physics course for high schools prepared by the Physical Science Study Committee, a course for which textbooks, laboratory exercises, films, and special teaching manuals have been prepared, as well as training courses for teachers. Some twenty-five thousand high school students are taking this course, and its impact is now being studied. There are similar projects in the field of mathematics under the supervision of the School Mathematics Study Group, the Commission on Mathematics, the University of Illinois Committee on School Mathematics, and other groups. The Biological Sciences Curriculum Study is constructing a high school biology course, and work of a comparable nature is under way in chemistry and other fields.

The main objective of this work has been to present subject matter effectively—that is, with due regard not only for coverage but also for structure. The daring and imagination that have gone into this work and the remarkable early successes it has achieved have stimulated psychologists who are concerned with the nature of learning and the transmission of knowledge. The Woods Hole Conference, the background and conduct of which are described in the Preface, was one response to this stimulation of interest. Physicists, biologists, mathematicians, historians, educators, and psychologists came together to consider anew the nature of the learning process, its relevance to education, and points at which current curricular efforts have raised new questions about our conceptions of learning and teaching. What shall be taught, when, and how? What kinds of research and inquiry might further the growing effort in the design of curricula? What are the implications of emphasizing the structure of a subject, be it mathematics or history—emphasizing it in a way that seeks to give a student as quickly as possible a sense of the fundamental ideas of a discipline?

An additional word of background is needed to appreciate the significance of present curricular efforts in the changing educational scene. The past half century has witnessed the rise of the American university graduate school with its strong emphasis upon advanced study and research. One consequence of this development has been the growing separation of first-rank scholars and scientists from the task of presenting their own subjects in primary and secondary schools—indeed even in elementary courses for undergraduates. The chief contact between those on the frontiers of scholarship and students in schools was through the occasional textbooks for high schools prepared by such distinguished scientists as Millikan or by historians of the stature of Beard or Commager. For the most part, however, the scholars at the forefront of their disciplines, those who might be able to make the greatest contribution to the substantive reorganization of their fields, were not involved in the development of curricula for the elementary and secondary schools. In consequence, school programs have often dealt inadequately or incorrectly with contemporary knowledge, and we have not reaped the benefits that might have come from a joining of the efforts of eminent scholars, wise and skillful teachers, and those trained in the fields related to teaching and learning. Now there appears to be a reversal of this trend. It consists in the renewed involvement of many of America's most distinguished scientists in the planning of school study programs in their field, in the preparation of textbooks and laboratory demonstrations, in the construction of films and television programs.

This same half century saw American psychology move away from its earlier concern with the nature of learning as it occurs in school. The psychology of learning tended to become involved with the precise details of learning in highly simplified short-term situations and thereby lost much of its contact with the long-term educational effects of learning. For their part, educational psychologists turned their attention with great effect to the study of aptitude and achievement and to social and motivational aspects of education, but did not concern themselves directly with the intellectual structure of class activities.

Other considerations led to a neglect of curriculum problems by psychologists. The ever-changing pattern of American educational philosophy played a part in the matter as well. There has always been a dualism in our educational ideal, a striving for a balance between what Benjamin Franklin referred to as the "useful" and the "ornamental." As he put it, in the mid-eighteenth century: "It would be well if they could be taught everything that is useful and everything that is orna-mental: but art is long and their time is short. It is there-fore proposed that they learn those things that are likely to be most useful and most ornamental." The concept of the useful in Franklin and in the American educational ideal afterwards was twofold: it involved, on the one hand, *skills* of a specific kind and, on the other, *general understanding*, to enable one better to deal with the affairs of life. Skills were matters of direct concern to one's profession. As early as the 1750's we find Ben Franklin urging that future merchants be taught French, German, and Spanish, and that pupils be taught agriculture, supplemented by farm visits and the like. General understanding was to be achieved through a knowledge of history plus the discipline produced by the diligent study of mathematics and logic, and by training in careful observation of the natural world around one; it required a well-disciplined, well-stocked mind.

The American secondary school has tried to strike a balance between the two concepts of usefulness—and most often with some regard for the ornamental as well. But as the proportion of the population registered in secondary schools increased, and as the proportion of new Americans in the school population went up, the balance between instruction in the useful skills and in disciplined understanding was harder to maintain. Dr. Conant's recent plea for the comprehensive high school is addressed to the problem of that balance.

It is interesting that around the turn of the last century the conception of the learning process as depicted by psychology gradually shifted away from an emphasis upon the production of general understanding to an emphasis on the acquisition of specific skills. The study of "transfer" provides the type case—the problem of the gain in mastery of other activities that one achieves from having mastered a particular learning task. Whereas the earlier emphasis had led to research studies on the transfer of formal discipline—the value obtained from the training of such "faculties" as analysis, judgment, memory, and so forth—later work tended to explore the transfer of identical elements or specific skills. In consequence, there was relatively little work by American psychologists during the first four decades of this century on the manner in which the student could be trained to grasp the underlying structure or significance of complex knowledge. Virtually all of the evidence of the last two decades on the nature of learning and transfer has indicated that, while the original theory of formal discipline was poorly stated in terms of the training of faculties, it is indeed a fact that massive general transfer can be achieved by appropriate learning, even to the degree that learning properly under optimum conditions leads one to "learn how to learn." These studies have stimulated a renewed interest in complex learning of a kind that one finds in schools, learning designed to produce general understanding of the structure of a subject matter. Interest in curricular problems at large has, in consequence, been rekindled among psychologists concerned with the learning process.

A word is needed at this point to explain in fuller detail what is meant by the *structure* of a subject, for we shall have occasion to return to this idea often in later pages. Three simple examples—from biology, from mathematics, and from the learning of language—help to make the idea clearer. Take first a set of observations on an inchworm crossing a sheet of graph paper mounted on a board. The board is horizontal; the animal moves in a straight line. We tilt the board so that the inclined plane or upward grade is 30°. The animal does not go straight up the line of maximum climb, but travels at an angle of 45° from it. We tilt the board to 60°. At what angle does the animal travel with respect to the line of maximum climb? His path now makes a 67½° angle with it, that is, he travels along a line 75° off the vertical. We may thus infer that inchworms "prefer" to travel uphill, if uphill they must go, along an incline of 15°. We have discovered a tropism, as it is called, indeed a geotropism. It is not an isolated fact. We can go on to show that among simple organisms, such phenomena—regulation of locomotion according to a fixed or built-in standard—are the rule. There is a preferred level of illumination toward which lower organisms orient, a preferred level of salinity, of temperature, and so on. Once a student grasps this basic relation between external stimulation and locomotor action, he is well on his way toward being able to handle a good deal of seemingly new but, in fact, highly related information. The swarming of locusts where temperature determines the swarm density in which locusts are forced to travel, the species maintenance of insects at different altitudes on the side of a mountain where crossbreeding is prevented by the tendency of each species to travel in its preferred oxygen zone, and many other phenomena in biology can be understood in the light of tropisms. Grasping the structure of a subject is understanding it in a way that permits many other things to be related to it meaningfully. To learn structure, in short, is to learn how things are related.

Much more briefly, to take an example from mathematics, algebra is a way of arranging knowns and unknowns in equations so that the unknowns are made knowable. The three fundamentals involved in working with these equations are commutation, distribution, and association. Once a student grasps the ideas embodied by these three fundamentals, he is in a position to recognize wherein "new" equations to be solved are not new at all, but variants on a familiar theme. Whether the student knows the formal names of these operations is less important for transfer than whether he is able to use them.

The often unconscious nature of learning structures is perhaps best illustrated in learning one's native language. Having grasped the subtle structure of a sentence, the child very rapidly learns to generate many other sentences based on this model though different in content from the original sentence learned. And having mastered the rules for transforming sentences without altering their meaning—"The dog bit the man" and "The man was bitten by the dog"—the child is able to vary his sentences much more widely. Yet, while young children are able to *use* the structural rules of English, they are certainly not able to say what the rules are.

The scientists constructing curricula in physics and mathematics have been highly mindful of the problem of teaching the structure of their subjects, and it may be that their early successes have been due to this emphasis. Their emphasis upon structure has stimulated students of the learning process. The reader will find the emphasis reflected many times in the pages that follow.

Clearly there are general questions to be faced before one can look at specific problems of courses, sequences, and the like. The moment one begins to ask questions about the value of specific courses, one is asking about the objectives of education. The construction of curricula proceeds in a world where changing social, cultural, and political conditions continually alter the surroundings and the goals of schools and their students. We are concerned with curricula designed for Americans, for their ways and their needs in a complex world. Americans are a changing people; their geographical mobility makes imperative some degree of uniformity among high schools and primary schools. Yet the diversity of American communities and of American life in general makes equally imperative some degree of variety in curricula. And whatever the limits placed on education by the demands of diversity and uniformity, there are also requirements for productivity to be met: are we producing enough scholars, scientists, poets, lawmakers, to meet the demands of our times? Moreover, schools must also contribute to the social and emotional development of the child if they are to fulfill their function of education for life in a democratic community and for fruitful family life. If the emphasis in what follows is principally on the intellectual side of education, it is not that the other objectives of education are less important.

We may take as perhaps the most general objective of education that it cultivate excellence; but it should be clear in what sense this phrase is used. It here refers not only to schooling the better student but also to helping each student achieve his optimum intellectual development. Good teaching that emphasizes the structure of a subject is probably even more valuable for the less able student than for the gifted one, for it is the former rather than the latter who is most easily thrown off the track by poor teaching. This is not to say that the pace or the content of courses need be identical for all students—though, as one member of the Conference put it, "When you teach well, it always seems as if seventy-five per cent of the students are above the median." Careful investigation and research can tell us wherein differences must be introduced. One thing seems clear: if all students are helped to the full utilization of their intellectual powers, we will have a better chance of surviving as a democracy in an age of enormous technological and social complexity.

The chapters that follow will be found to be somewhat specialized in the direction of the sciences and mathematics and how they might best be taught. This should not be taken as a declaration in favor of emphasizing the sciences and scientific training. It is an accident, rather, of historical developments over the last ten years. There has simply been more opportunity to examine progress in these fields, since it is in these fields that most of the experimental curricula have been constructed. Redoubled efforts are essential in the social studies, in the humanities, and in language instruction. A sense of tragedy and triumph achieved through the study of history and literature is surely as important to modern man as a sense of the structure of matter achieved through the study of physics. It should be utterly clear that the humanities, the social studies, and the sciences are all equally in need of imaginative effort if they are to make their proper contribution to the education of coming generations.

The top quarter of public school students, from which we must draw intellectual leadership in the next generation, is perhaps the group most neglected by our schools in the recent past. Improvements in the teaching of science and mathematics may very well accentuate the gaps already observable between talented, average, and slow students in these subjects. Even as they now exist, these gaps raise difficult problems. It is plain that, in general, scientific and mathematical aptitudes can be discovered earlier than other intellectual talents. Ideally, schools should allow students to go ahead in different subjects as rapidly as they can. But the administrative problems that are raised when one makes such an arrangement possible are almost inevitably beyond the resources that schools have available for dealing with them. The answer will probably lie in some modification or abolition of the system of grade levels in some subjects, notably mathematics, along with a program of course enrichment in other subjects. Questions about the enrichment and the special handling of gifted students will doubtless persuade the more enlightened and wealthier schools to modify current practices. But we can certainly ill afford as a nation to allow local inadequacies to inhibit the development of children born into relatively poor towns or regions.

Four themes are developed in the chapters that follow. The first of these has already been introduced: the role of structure in learning and how it may be made central in teaching. The approach taken is a practical one. Students, perforce, have a limited exposure to the materials they are to learn. How can this exposure be made to count in their thinking for the rest of their lives? The dominant view among men who have been engaged in preparing and teaching new curricula is that the answer to this question lies in giving students an understanding of the fundamental structure of whatever subjects we choose to teach. This is a minimum requirement for using knowledge, for bringing it to bear on problems and events one encounters outside a classroom—or in classrooms one enters later in one's training. The teaching and learning of structure, rather than simply the mastery of facts and techniques, is at the center of the classic problem of transfer. There are many things that go into learning of this kind, not the least of which are supporting habits and skills that make possible the active use of the materials one has come to understand. If earlier learning is to render later learning easier, it must do so by providing a general picture in terms of which the relations between things encountered earlier and later are made as clear as possible.

Given the importance of this theme, much too little is known about how to teach fundamental structure effectively or how to provide learning conditions that foster it. Much of the discussion in the chapter devoted to this topic has to do with ways and means of achieving such teaching and learning and with the kinds of research needed to help in preparing curricula with emphasis on structure.

The second theme has to do with readiness for learning. Experience over the past decade points to the fact that our schools may be wasting precious years by postponing the teaching of many important subjects on the ground that they are too difficult. The reader will find the chapter devoted to this theme introduced by the proposition that the foundations of any subject may be taught to anybody at any age in some form. Though the proposition may seem startling at first, its intent is to underscore an essential point often overlooked in the planning of curricula. It is that the basic ideas that lie at the heart of all science and mathematics and the basic themes that give form to life and literature are as simple

as they are powerful. To be in command of these basic
ideas, to use them effectively, requires a continual deepening of one's understanding of them that comes from
learning to use them in progressively more complex
forms. It is only when such basic ideas are put in formalized terms as equations or elaborated verbal concepts
that they are out of reach of the young child, if he has
not first understood them intuitively and had a chance
to try them out on his own. The early teaching of science, mathematics, social studies, and literature should
be designed to teach these subjects with scrupulous intellectual honesty, but with an emphasis upon the intuitive grasp of ideas and upon the use of these basic ideas.
A curriculum as it develops should revisit these basic
ideas repeatedly, building upon them until the student
has grasped the full formal apparatus that goes with
them. Fourth-grade children can play absorbing games
governed by the principles of topology and set theory,
even discovering new "moves" or theorems. They can
grasp the idea of tragedy and the basic human plights
represented in myth. But they cannot put these ideas
into formal language or manipulate them as grownups
can. There is much still to be learned about the "spiral
curriculum" that turns back on itself at higher levels,
and many questions still to be answered are discussed in
Chapter 3.

The third theme involves the nature of intuition—the
intellectual technique of arriving at plausible but tentative formulations without going through the analytic
steps by which such formulations would be found to be
valid or invalid conclusions. Intuitive thinking, the training of hunches, is a much-neglected and essential feature

of productive thinking not only in formal academic disciplines but also in everyday life. The shrewd guess, the fertile hypothesis, the courageous leap to a tentative conclusion—these are the most valuable coin of the thinker at work, whatever his line of work. Can school children be led to master this gift?

The three themes mentioned so far are all premised on a central conviction: that intellectual activity anywhere is the same, whether at the frontier of knowledge or in a third-grade classroom. What a scientist does at his desk or in his laboratory, what a literary critic does in reading a poem, are of the same order as what anybody else does when he is engaged in like activities—if he is to achieve understanding. The difference is in degree, not in kind. The schoolboy learning physics *is* a physicist, and it is easier for him to learn physics behaving like a physicist than doing something else. The "something else" usually involves the task of mastering what came to be called at Woods Hole a "middle language"—classroom discussions and textbooks that talk about the conclusions in a field of intellectual inquiry rather than centering upon the inquiry itself. Approached in that way, high school physics often looks very little like physics, social studies are removed from the issues of life and society as usually discussed, and school mathematics too often has lost contact with what is at the heart of the subject, the idea of order.

The fourth theme relates to the desire to learn and how it may be stimulated. Ideally, interest in the material to be learned is the best stimulus to learning, rather than such external goals as grades or later competitive advantage. While it is surely unrealistic to assume that the pressures of competition can be effectively eliminated or that it is wise to seek their elimination, it is nonetheless worth considering how interest in learning per se can be stimulated. There was much discussion at Woods Hole of how the climate in which school learning occurs can be improved, discussion that ranged over such diverse topics as teacher training, the nature of school examinations, the quality of a curriculum. Chapter 5 is devoted to this set of problems.

While there was considerable discussion at Woods Hole of the apparatus of teaching—films, television, and audio-visual aids, teaching machines, and other devices that a teacher may use in instruction—there was anything but consensus on the subject. Virtually all of the participants agreed that not teaching devices but teachers were the principal agents of instruction, but there was a division of opinion on how the teacher was to be aided. The disagreement, perhaps, can be summarized (though oversimplified in the process) in terms of the relative emphasis placed upon the teacher as such and upon the aids that the teacher might employ. The two extreme positions—stated in exaggerated form—were, first, that the teacher must be the sole and final arbiter of how to present a given subject and what devices to use, and, second, that the teacher should be explicator and commentator for prepared materials made available through films, television, teaching machines, and the like. The implication of the first extreme position is that every effort should be made to educate the teacher to a deep knowledge of his or her subject so that he or she may do as good a job as possible with it, and at the same time the best materials should be made available for the teacher to choose from in constructing a course that meets the requirements of the syllabus. The other extreme implies a massive effort to prepare films, television programs, instructional programs for teaching machines, and so on, and to teach the teacher how to use these with wisdom and understanding of the subject. The debate is sufficiently intense and its implications for a philosophy of education sufficiently great that the concluding chapter is devoted to this issue.

In sum, then, we shall concentrate on four themes and one conjecture: the themes of structure, readiness, intuition, and interest, and the conjecture of how best to aid the teacher in the task of instruction.

2

THE IMPORTANCE OF STRUCTURE

THE first object of any act of learning, over and beyond the pleasure it may give, is that it should serve us in the future. Learning should not only take us somewhere; it should allow us later to go further more easily. There are two ways in which learning serves the future. One is through its specific applicability to tasks that are highly similar to those we originally learned to perform. Psychologists refer to this phenomenon as specific transfer of training; perhaps it should be called the extension of habits or associations. Its utility appears to be limited in the main to what we usually speak of as skills. Having learned how to hammer nails, we are better able later to learn how to hammer tacks or chip wood. Learning in school undoubtedly creates skills of a kind that transfers to activities encountered later, either in school or after. A second way in which earlier learning renders later performance more efficient is through what is conveniently called nonspecific transfer or, more accurately, the transfer of principles and attitudes. In essence, it consists of learning initially not a skill but a general idea, which can then be used as a basis for recognizing subsequent problems as special cases of the idea originally mastered. This type of transfer is at the heart of the educational process—the continual broadening and deepening of knowledge in terms of basic and general ideas.

The continuity of learning that is produced by the second type of transfer, transfer of principles, is dependent upon mastery of the structure of the subject matter, as structure was described in the preceding chapter. That is to say, in order for a person to be able to recognize the applicability or inapplicability of an idea to a new situation and to broaden his learning thereby, he must have clearly in mind the general nature of the phenomenon with which he is dealing. The more fundamental or basic is the idea he has learned, almost by definition, the greater will be its breadth of applicability to new problems. Indeed, this is almost a tautology, for what is meant by "fundamental" in this sense is precisely that an idea has wide as well as powerful applicability. It is simple enough to proclaim, of course, that school curricula and methods of teaching should be geared to the teaching of fundamental ideas in whatever subject is being taught. But as soon as one makes such a statement a host of problems arise, many of which can be solved only with the aid of considerably more research. We turn to some of these now.

The first and most obvious problem is how to construct curricula that can be taught by ordinary teachers to ordinary students and that at the same time reflect clearly the basic or underlying principles of various fields of inquiry. The problem is twofold: first, how to have the basic subjects rewritten and their teaching materials revamped in such a way that the pervading and powerful ideas and attitudes relating to them are given a central role; second, how to match the levels of these materials to the capacities of students of different abilities at different grades in school.

The experience of the past several years has taught at least one important lesson about the design of a curriculum that is true to the underlying structure of its subject matter. It is that the best minds in any particular discipline must be put to work on the task. The decision as to what should be taught in American history to elementary school children or what should be taught in arithmetic is a decision that can best be reached with the aid of those with a high degree of vision and competence in each of these fields. To decide that the elementary ideas of algebra depend upon the fundamentals of the commutative, distributive, and associative laws, one must be a mathematician in a position to appreciate and understand the fundamentals of mathematics. Whether schoolchildren require an understanding of Frederick Jackson Turner's ideas about the role of the frontier in American history before they can sort out the facts and trends of American history—this again is a decision that requires the help of the scholar who has a deep understanding of the American past. Only by the use of our best minds in devising curricula will we bring the fruits of scholarship and wisdom to the student just beginning his studies.

The question will be raised, "How enlist the aid of our most able scholars and scientists in designing curricula for primary and secondary schools?" The answer has already been given, at least in part. The School Mathematics Study Group, the University of Illinois mathematics projects, the Physical Science Study Committee, and the Biological Sciences Curriculum Study have indeed been enlisting the aid of eminent men in their various fields, doing so by means of summer proj-

19

ects, supplemented in part by year-long leaves of absence for certain key people involved. They have been aided in these projects by outstanding elementary and secondary school teachers and, for special purposes, by professional writers, film makers, designers, and others required in such a complex enterprise.

There is at least one major matter that is left unsettled even by a large-scale revision of curricula in the direction indicated. Mastery of the fundamental ideas of a field involves not only the grasping of general principles, but also the development of an attitude toward learning and inquiry, toward guessing and hunches, toward the possibility of solving problems on one's own. Just as a physicist has certain attitudes about the ultimate orderliness of nature and a conviction that order can be discovered, so a young physics student needs some working version of these attitudes if he is to organize his learning in such a way as to make what he learns usable and meaningful in his thinking. To instill such attitudes by teaching requires something more than the mere presentation of fundamental ideas. Just what it takes to bring off such teaching is something on which a great deal of research is needed, but it would seem that an important ingredient is a sense of excitement about discovery—discovery of regularities of previously unrecognized relations and similarities between ideas, with a resulting sense of self-confidence in one's abilities. Various people who have worked on curricula in science and mathematics have urged that it is possible to present the fundamental structure of a discipline in such a way as to preserve some of the exciting sequences that lead a student to discover for himself.

It is particularly the Committee on School Mathematics and the Arithmetic Project of the University of Illinois that have emphasized the importance of discovery as an aid to teaching. They have been active in devising methods that permit a student to discover for himself the generalization that lies behind a particular mathematical operation, and they contrast this approach with the "method of assertion and proof" in which the generalization is first stated by the teacher and the class asked to proceed through the proof. It has also been pointed out by the Illinois group that the method of discovery would be too time-consuming for presenting all of what a student must cover in mathematics. The proper balance between the two is anything but plain, and research is in progress to elucidate the matter, though more is needed. Is the inductive approach a better technique for teaching principles? Does it have a desirable effect on attitudes?

That the method of discovery need not be limited to such highly formalized subjects as mathematics and physics is illustrated by some experimentation on social studies carried out by the Harvard Cognition Project. A sixth-grade class, having been through a conventional unit on the social and economic geography of the Southeastern states, was introduced to the North Central region by being asked to locate the major cities of the area on a map containing physical features and natural resources, but no place names. The resulting class discussion very rapidly produced a variety of plausible theories concerning the requirements of a city—a water transportation theory that placed Chicago at the junction of the three lakes, a mineral resources theory that placed

21

it near the Mesabi range, a food-supply theory that put a great city on the rich soil of Iowa, and so on. The level of interest as well as the level of conceptual sophistication was far above that of control classes. Most striking, however, was the attitude of children to whom, for the first time, the location of a city appeared as a problem, and one to which an answer could be discovered by taking thought. Not only was there pleasure and excitement in the pursuit of a question, but in the end the discovery was worth making, at least for urban children for whom the phenomenon of the city was something that had before been taken for granted.

How do we tailor fundamental knowledge to the interests and capacities of children? This is a theme we shall return to later, and only a word need be said about it here. It requires a combination of deep understanding and patient honesty to present physical or any other phenomena in a way that is simultaneously exciting, correct, and rewardingly comprehensible. In examining certain teaching materials in physics, for example, we have found much patient honesty in presentation that has come to naught because the authors did not have a deep enough understanding of the subject they were presenting.

A good case in point is to be found in the usual attempt to explain the nature of tides. Ask the majority of high school students to explain tides and they will speak of the gravitational pull of the moon on the surface of the earth and how it pulls the water on the moon's side into a bulge. Ask them now why there is also a bulge of less magnitude on the side of the earth opposite to the moon, and they will almost always be without a satisfactory answer. Or ask them where the maximum bulge of the incoming tide is with respect to the relative position of the earth and moon, and the answer will usually be that it is at the point on the earth's surface nearest to the moon. If the student knows there is a lag in the tidal crest, he will usually not know why. The failure in both cases comes from an inadequate picture of how gravity acts upon a free-moving elastic body, and a failure to connect the idea of inertia with the idea of gravitational action. In short, the tides are explained without a share of the excitement that can come from understanding Newton's great discovery of universal gravitation and its mode of action. Correct and illuminating explanations are no more difficult and often easier to grasp than ones that are partly correct and therefore too complicated and too restricted. It is the consensus of virtually all the men and women who have been working on curriculum projects that making material interesting is in no way incompatible with presenting it soundly; indeed, a correct general explanation is often the most interesting of all. Inherent in the preceding discussions are at least four general claims that can be made for teaching the fundamental structure of a subject, claims in need of detailed study.

The first is that understanding fundamentals makes a subject more comprehensible. This is true not only in physics and mathematics, where we have principally illustrated the point, but equally in the social studies and literature. Once one has grasped the fundamental idea that a nation must trade in order to live, then such a presumably special phenomenon as the Triangular Trade of the American colonies becomes altogether simpler to understand as something more than commerce in molasses, sugar cane, rum, and slaves in an atmosphere of violation of British trade regulations. The high school student reading *Moby Dick* can only understand more deeply if he can be led to understand that Melville's novel is, among other things, a study of the theme of evil and the plight of those pursuing this "killing whale." And if the student is led further to understand that there are a relatively limited number of human plights about which novels are written, he understands literature the better for it.

The second point relates to human memory. Perhaps the most basic thing that can be said about human memory, after a century of intensive research, is that unless detail is placed into a structured pattern, it is rapidly forgotten. Detailed material is conserved in memory by the use of simplified ways of representing it. These simplified representations have what may be called a "regenerative" character. A good example of this regenerative property of long-term memory can be found in science. A scientist does not try to remember the distances traversed by falling bodies in different gravitational fields over different periods of time. What he carries in memory instead is a formula that permits him with varying degrees of accuracy to regenerate the details on which the more easily remembered formula is based. So he commits to memory the formula $s = \frac{1}{2} gt^2$ and not a handbook of distances, times, and gravitational constants. Similarly, one does not remember exactly what Marlowe, the commentator in *Lord Jim*, said about the chief protagonist's plight, but, rather, simply that he was the dispassionate onlooker, the man who tried to understand without judging what had led Lord Jim into the straits in which he found himself. We remember a formula, a vivid detail that carries the meaning of an event, an average that stands for a range of events, a caricature or picture that preserves an essence—all of them techniques of condensation and representation. What learning general or fundamental principles does is to ensure that memory loss will not mean total loss, that what remains will permit us to reconstruct the details when needed. A good theory is the vehicle not only for understanding a phenomenon now but also for remembering it tomorrow.

Third, an understanding of fundamental principles and ideas, as noted earlier, appears to be the main road to adequate "transfer of training." To understand something as a specific instance of a more general case—which is what understanding a more fundamental principle or structure means—is to have learned not only a specific thing but also a model for understanding other things like it that one may encounter. If a student could grasp in its most human sense the weariness of Europe at the close of the Thirty Years' War and how it created the conditions for a workable but not ideologically absolute Treaty of Westphalia, he might be better able to think about the ideological struggle of East and West—though the parallel is anything but exact. A carefully wrought understanding should also permit him to recognize the limits of the generalization as well. The idea of "principles" and "concepts" as a basis for transfer is hardly new. It is much in need of more research of a specific kind that would provide detailed knowledge of how best to proceed in the teaching of different subjects in different grades.

The fourth claim for emphasis on structure and principles in teaching is that by constantly reexamining material taught in elementary and secondary schools for its fundamental character, one is able to narrow the gap between "advanced" knowledge and "elementary" knowledge. Part of the difficulty now found in the progression from primary school through high school to college is that material learned earlier is either out of date or misleading by virtue of its lagging too far behind developments in a field. This gap can be reduced by the kind of emphasis set forth in the preceding discussion.

Consider now some specific problems that received considerable discussion at Woods Hole. One of them has to do with the troubled topic of "general science." There are certain recurrent ideas that appear in virtually all branches of science. If in one subject one has learned them well and generally, that achievement should make the task of learning them again in different form elsewhere in science much easier. Various teachers and scientists have raised the question whether these basic ideas should not be "isolated," so to speak, and taught more explicitly in a manner that frees them from specific areas of science. The type of idea can be easily illustrated: categorization and its uses, the unit of measure and its development, the indirectness of information in science and the need for operational definition of ideas, and so forth. With respect to the last, for example, we do not *see* pressure or the chemical bond directly but infer it indirectly from a set of measures. So too body temperature. So too sadness in another person. Can these and similar ideas be presented effectively and with a variety of concrete illustrations in the early grades in order to give the child a better basis for understanding their specific representation in various special disciplines later? Is it wise to teach such "general science" as an introduction to disciplinary sciences in the later grades? How should they be taught and what could we reasonably expect by way of easier learning later? Much research is needed on this promising topic—research not only on the usefulness of such an approach, but also on the kinds of general scientific ideas that might be taught.

Indeed, it may well be that there are certain general attitudes or approaches toward science or literature that can be taught in the earlier grades that would have considerable relevance for later learning. The attitude that things are connected and not isolated is a case in point. One can indeed imagine kindergarten games designed to make children more actively alert to how things affect or are connected with each other—a kind of introduction to the idea of multiple determination of events in the physical and the social world. Any working scientist is usually able to say something about the ways of thinking or attitudes that are a part of his craft. Historians have written rather extensively on this subject as far as their field is concerned. Literary men have even evolved a genre of writing about the forms of sensibility that make for literary taste and vigor. In mathematics, this subject has a formal name, "heuristic," to describe the approach one takes to solving problems. One may well argue, as it was argued at Woods Hole by men in widely differing disciplines, that it might be wise to assess what attitudes or heuristic devices are most pervasive and useful, and that an effort should be made to teach children a rudimentary version of them that might be further refined as they progress through school. Again, the reader will sense that the argument for such an approach is premised on the assumption that there is a continuity between what a scholar does on the forefront of his discipline and what a child does in approaching it for the first time. This is not to say that the task is a simple one, only that it is worthy of careful consideration and research.

Perhaps the chief arguments put forward in opposition to the idea of such efforts at teaching general principles and general attitudes are, first, that it is better to approach the general through the specific and, second, that working attitudes should be kept implicit rather than being made explicit. For example, one of the principal organizing concepts in biology is the persistent question, "What function does this thing serve?"—a question premised on the assumption that everything one finds in an organism serves some function or it probably would not have survived. Other general ideas are related to this question. The student who makes progress in biology learns to ask the question more and more subtly, to relate more and more things to it. At the next step he asks what function a particular structure or process serves in the light of what is required in the total functioning of an organism. Measuring and categorizing are carried out in the service of the general idea of function. Then beyond that he may organize his knowledge in terms of a still more comprehensive notion of function, turning to cellular structure or to phylogenetic comparison. It may well be that the style of thought of a particular discipline is necessary as a background for learning the working meaning of general concepts, in which case a general introduction to the meaning of "function" might be less effective than teaching it in the context of biology.

As for "attitude" teaching or even the teaching of heuristic in mathematics, the argument runs that if the learner becomes too aware of his own attitudes or approach, he may become mechanical or trick-oriented in his work. No evidence exists on the point, and research is needed before any effort is made to teach in this way. Work is now going on at Illinois on training children to be more effective in asking questions about physical phenomena, but much more information is needed before the issue is clear.

One hears often the distinction between "doing" and "understanding." It is a distinction applied to the case, for example, of a student who presumably understands a mathematical idea but does not know how to use it in computation. While the distinction is probably a false one—since how can one know what a student understands save by seeing what he does—it points to an interesting difference in emphasis in teaching and in learning. Thus one finds in some of the classic books on the psychology of problem solving (such as Max Wertheimer's *Productive Thinking*) a sharp line drawn between "rote drill" and "understanding." In point of fact, drill need not be rote and, alas, emphasis on understanding may lead the student to a certain verbal glibness. It has been the experience of members of the School Mathematics Study Group that computational practice may be a necessary step toward understanding conceptual ideas in mathematics. Similarly one may try to give the high school student a sense of styles by having him read contrasting authors, yet final insight into style may come only when the student himself tries his hand at writing in different styles. Indeed, it is the underlying premise of laboratory exercises that doing something helps one understand it. There is a certain wisdom in the quip made by a psychologist at Woods Hole: "How do I know what I think until I feel what I do?" In any case, the distinction is not a very helpful one. What is more to the point is to ask what methods of exercise in any given field are most likely to give the student a sense of intelligent mastery over the material. What are the most fruitful computational exercises that one can use in various branches of mathematics? Does the effort to write in the style of Henry James give one an especially good insight into that author's style? Perhaps a good start toward understanding such matters would be to study the methods used by successful teachers. It would be surprising if the information compiled failed to suggest a host of worthwhile laboratory studies on techniques of teaching—or, indeed, on techniques of imparting complex information generally.

A word is needed, finally, on examinations. It is obvious that an examination can be bad in the sense of emphasizing trivial aspects of a subject. Such examinations can encourage teaching in a disconnected fashion and learning by rote. What is often overlooked, however, is that examinations can also be allies in the battle to improve curricula and teaching. Whether an examination is of the "objective" type involving multiple choices or of the essay type, it can be devised so as to emphasize an understanding of the broad principles of a subject. Indeed, even when one examines on detailed knowledge, it can be done in such a way as to require an understanding by the student of the connectedness between specific facts. There is a concerted effort now under way among national testing organizations like the Educational Testing Service to construct examinations that will emphasize an understanding of fundamental principles. Such efforts can be of great help. Additional help might be given to local school systems by making available to them manuals that describe the variety of ways in which examinations can be constructed. The searching examination is not easy to make, and a thoughtful manual on the subject would be welcome.

To recapitulate, the main theme of this chapter has been that the curriculum of a subject should be determined by the most fundamental understanding that can be achieved of the underlying principles that give structure to that subject. Teaching specific topics or skills without making clear their context in the broader fundamental structure of a field of knowledge is uneconomical in several deep senses. In the first place, such teaching makes it exceedingly difficult for the student to generalize from what he has learned to what he will encounter later. In the second place, learning that has fallen short of a grasp of general principles has little reward in terms of intellectual excitement. The best way to create interest in a subject is to render it worth knowing, which means to make the knowledge gained usable in one's thinking beyond the situation in which the learning has occurred. Third, knowledge one has acquired without sufficient structure to tie it together is knowledge that is likely to be forgotten. An unconnected set of facts has a pitiably short half-life in memory. Organizing facts in terms of principles and ideas from which they may be inferred is the only known way of reducing the quick rate of loss of human memory.

Designing curricula in a way that reflects the basic structure of a field of knowledge requires the most fundamental understanding of that field. It is a task that cannot be carried out without the active participation of the ablest scholars and scientists. The experience of the past several years has shown that such scholars and scientists, working in conjunction with experienced teachers and students of child development, can prepare curricula of the sort we have been considering. Much more effort in the actual preparation of curriculum materials, in teacher training, and in supporting research will be necessary if improvements in our educational practices are to be of an order that will meet the challenges of the scientific and social revolution through which we are now living.

There are many problems of how to teach general principles in a way that will be both effective and interesting, and several of the key issues have been passed in review. What is abundantly clear is that much work remains to be done by way of examining currently effective practices, fashioning curricula that may be tried out on an experimental basis, and carrying out the kinds of research that can give support and guidance to the general effort at improving teaching.

How may the kind of curriculum we have been discussing be brought within the intellectual reach of children of different ages? To this problem we turn next.

3

READINESS FOR LEARNING

W E begin with the hypothesis that any subject can be taught effectively in some intellectually honest form to any child at any stage of development. It is a bold hypothesis and an essential one in thinking about the nature of a curriculum. No evidence exists to contradict it; considerable evidence is being amassed that supports it.

To make clear what is implied, let us examine three general ideas. The first has to do with the process of intellectual development in children, the second with the act of learning, and the third with the notion of the "spiral curriculum" introduced earlier.

Intellectual development. Research on the intellectual development of the child highlights the fact that at each stage of development the child has a characteristic way of viewing the world and explaining it to himself. The task of teaching a subject to a child at any particular age is one of representing the structure of that subject in terms of the child's way of viewing things. The task can be thought of as one of translation. The general hypothesis that has just been stated is premised on the considered judgment that any idea can be represented honestly and usefully in the thought forms of children of school age, and that these first representations can later be made more powerful and precise the more easily by virtue of this early learning. To illustrate and support this view, we present here a somewhat detailed picture of the course of intellectual development, along with some suggestions about teaching at different stages of it.

The work of Piaget and others suggests that, roughly speaking, one may distinguish three stages in the intellectual development of the child. The first stage need not concern us in detail, for it is characteristic principally of the pre-school child. In this stage, which ends (at least for Swiss school children) around the fifth or sixth year, the child's mental work consists principally in establishing relationships between experience and action; his concern is with manipulating the world through action. This stage corresponds roughly to the period from the first development of language to the point at which the child learns to manipulate symbols. In this so-called preoperational stage, the principal symbolic achievement is that the child learns how to represent the external world through symbols established by simple generalization; things are represented as equivalent in terms of sharing some common property. But the child's symbolic world does not make a clear separation between internal motives and feelings on the one hand and external reality on the other. The sun moves because God pushes it, and the stars, like himself, have to go to bed. The child is little able to separate his own goals from the means for achieving them, and when he has to make corrections in his activity after unsuccessful attempts at manipulating reality, he does so by what are called intuitive regulations rather than by symbolic operations, the former being of a crude trial-and-error nature rather than the result of taking thought.

What is principally lacking at this stage of development is what the Geneva school has called the concept of reversibility. When the shape of an object is changed, as when one changes the shape of a ball of plasticene, the preoperational child cannot grasp the idea that it can be brought back readily to its original state. Because of this fundamental lack the child cannot understand certain fundamental ideas that lie at the basis of mathematics and physics—the mathematical idea that one conserves quantity even when one partitions a set of things into subgroups, or the physical idea that one conserves mass and weight even though one transforms the shape of an object. It goes without saying that teachers are severely limited in transmitting concepts to a child at this stage, even in a highly intuitive manner.

The second stage of development—and now the child is in school—is called the stage of concrete operations. This stage is operational in contrast to the preceding stage, which is merely active. An operation is a type of action: it can be carried out rather directly by the manipulation of objects, or internally, as when one manipulates the symbols that represent things and relations in one's mind. Roughly, an operation is a means of getting data about the real world into the mind and there transforming them so that they can be organized and used selectively in the solution of problems. Assume a child is presented with a pinball machine which bounces a ball off a wall at an angle. Let us find out what he appreciates about the relation between the angle of incidence and the angle of reflection. The young child sees no problem: for him, the ball travels in an arc, touching the wall on the way. The somewhat older child, say age ten, sees the two angles as roughly related

—as one changes so does the other. The still older child begins to grasp that there is a fixed relation between the two, and usually says it is a right angle. Finally, the thirteen- or fourteen-year-old, often by pointing the ejector directly at the wall and seeing the ball come back at the ejector, gets the idea that the two angles are equal. Each way of looking at the phenomenon represents the result of an operation in this sense, and the child's thinking is constrained by his way of pulling his observations together.

An operation differs from simple action or goal-directed behavior in that it is internalized and reversible. "Internalized" means that the child does not have to go about his problem-solving any longer by overt trial and error, but can actually carry out trial and error in his head. Reversibility is present because operations are seen as characterized where appropriate by what is called "complete compensation"; that is to say, an operation can be compensated for by an inverse operation. If marbles, for example, are divided into subgroups, the child can grasp intuitively that the original collection of marbles can be restored by being added back together again. The child tips a balance scale too far with a weight and then searches systematically for a lighter weight or for something with which to get the scale rebalanced. He may carry reversibility too far by assuming that a piece of paper, once burned, can also be restored.

With the advent of concrete operations, the child develops an internalized structure with which to operate. In the example of the balance scale, the structure is a serial order of weights that the child has in his mind.

Such internal structures are of the essence. They are the internalized symbolic systems by which the child represents the world, as in the example of the pinball machine and the angles of incidence and reflection. It is into the language of these internal structures that one must translate ideas if the child is to grasp them.

But concrete operations, though they are guided by the logic of classes and the logic of relations, are means for structuring only immediately present reality. The child is able to give structure to the things he encounters, but he is not yet readily able to deal with possibilities not directly before him or not already experienced. This is not to say that children operating concretely are not able to anticipate things that are not present. Rather, it is that they do not command the operations for conjuring up systematically the full range of alternative possibilities that could exist at any given time. They cannot go systematically beyond the information given them to a description of what else might occur. Somewhere between ten and fourteen years of age the child passes into a third stage, which is called the stage of "formal operations" by the Geneva school.

Now the child's intellectual activity seems to be based upon an ability to operate on hypothetical propositions rather than being constrained to what he has experienced or what is before him. The child can now think of possible variables and even deduce potential relationships that can later be verified by experiment or observation. Intellectual operations now appear to be predicated upon the same kinds of logical operations that are the stock in trade of the logician, the scientist, or the abstract thinker. It is at this point that the child is able to give formal or axiomatic expression to the concrete ideas that before guided his problem-solving but could not be described or formally understood.

Earlier, while the child is in the stage of concrete operations, he is capable of grasping intuitively and concretely a great many of the basic ideas of mathematics, the sciences, the humanities, and the social sciences. But he can do so only in terms of concrete operations. It can be demonstrated that fifth-grade children can play mathematical games with rules modeled on highly advanced mathematics; indeed, they can arrive at these rules inductively and learn how to work with them. They will flounder, however, if one attempts to force upon them a formal mathematical description of what they have been doing, though they are perfectly capable of guiding their behavior by these rules. At the Woods Hole Conference we were privileged to see a demonstration of teaching in which fifth-grade children very rapidly grasped central ideas from the theory of functions, although had the teacher attempted to explain to them what the theory of functions was, he would have drawn a blank. Later, at the appropriate stage of development and given a certain amount of practice in concrete operations, the time would be ripe for introducing them to the necessary formalism.

What is most important for teaching basic concepts is that the child be helped to pass progressively from concrete thinking to the utilization of more conceptually adequate modes of thought. But it is futile to attempt this by presenting formal explanations based on a logic that is distant from the child's manner of thinking and sterile in its implications for him. Much teaching in mathematics is of this sort. The child learns not to understand mathematical order but rather to apply certain devices or recipes without understanding their significance and connectedness. They are not translated into his way of thinking. Given this inappropriate start, he is easily led to believe that the important thing is for him to be "accurate"—though accuracy has less to do with mathematics than with computation. Perhaps the most striking example of this type of thing is to be found in the manner in which the high school student meets Euclidian geometry for the first time, as a set of axioms and theorems, without having had some experience with simple geometric configurations and the intuitive means whereby one deals with them. If the child were earlier given the concepts and strategies in the form of intuitive geometry at a level that he could easily follow, he might be far better able to grasp deeply the meaning of the theorems and axioms to which he is exposed later.

But the intellectual development of the child is no clockwork sequence of events; it also responds to influences from the environment, notably the school environment. Thus instruction in scientific ideas, even at the elementary level, need not follow slavishly the natural course of cognitive development in the child. It can also lead intellectual development by providing challenging but usable opportunities for the child to forge ahead in his development. Experience has shown that it is worth the effort to provide the growing child with problems that tempt him into next stages of development. As David Page, one of the most experienced teachers of elementary mathematics, has commented: "In teaching from kindergarten to graduate school, I have been amazed at the intellectual similarity of human beings at all ages, although children are perhaps more spontaneous, creative, and energetic than adults. As far as I am concerned young children learn almost anything faster than adults do if it can be given to them in terms they understand. Giving the material to them in terms they understand, interestingly enough, turns out to involve knowing the mathematics oneself, and the better one knows it, the better it can be taught. It is appropriate that we warn ourselves to be careful of assigning an absolute level of difficulty to any particular topic. When I tell mathematicians that fourth-grade students can go a long way into 'set theory' a few of them reply: 'Of course.' Most of them are startled. The latter ones are completely wrong in assuming that 'set theory' is intrinsically difficult. Of course it may be that nothing is intrinsically difficult. We just have to wait until the proper point of view and corresponding language for presenting it are revealed. Given particular subject matter or a particular concept, it is easy to ask trivial questions or to lead the child to ask trivial questions. It is also easy to ask impossibly difficult questions. The trick is to find the medium questions that can be answered and that take you somewhere. This is the big job of teachers and textbooks." One leads the child by the well-wrought "medium questions" to move more rapidly through the stages of intellectual development, to a deeper understanding of mathematical, physical, and historical principles. We must know far more about the ways in which this can be done.

Professor Inhelder of Geneva was asked to suggest ways in which the child could be moved along faster through the various stages of intellectual development in mathematics and physics. What follows is part of a memorandum she prepared for the Conference.

"The most elementary forms of reasoning—whether logical, arithmetical, geometrical, or physical—rest on the principle of the invariance of quantities: that the whole remains, whatever may be the arrangement of its parts, the change of its form, or its displacement in space or time. The principle of invariance is no a priori datum of the mind, nor is it the product of purely empirical observation. The child discovers invariance in a manner comparable to scientific discoveries generally. Grasping the idea of invariance is beset with difficulties for the child, often unsuspected by teachers. To the young child, numerical wholes, spatial dimensions, and physical quantities do not seem to remain constant but to dilate or contract as they are operated upon. The total number of beads in a box remains the same whether subdivided into two, three, or ten piles. It is this that is so hard for the child to understand. The young child perceives changes as operating in one direction without being able to grasp the idea that certain fundamental features of things remain constant over change, or that if they change the change is reversible.

"A few examples among many used in studying the child's concept of invariance will illustrate the kinds of materials one could use to help him to learn the concept more easily. The child transfers beads of a known quantity or liquids of a known volume from one receptacle to another, one receptacle being tall and narrow, the other flat and wide. The young child believes there is more in the tall receptacle than the flat one. Now the child can be confronted concretely with the nature of one-to-one correspondence between two versions of the same quantity. For there is an easy technique of checking: the beads can be counted or the liquid measured in some standard way. The same operations work for the conservation of spatial quantity if one uses a set of sticks for length or a set of tiles for surface, or by having the child transform the shape of volumes made up of the same number of blocks. In physics dissolving sugar or transforming the shapes of balls of plasticene while conserving volume provides comparable instruction. If teaching fails to bring the child properly from his perceptual, primitive notions to a proper intuition of the idea of invariance, the result is that he will count without having acquired the idea of the invariance of numerical quantities. Or he will use geometrical measures while remaining ignorant of the operation of transitivity—that if A includes B, and B includes C, then A also includes C. In physics he will apply calculations to imperfectly understood physical notions such as weight, volume, speed, and time. A teaching method that takes into account the natural thought processes will allow the child to discover such principles of invariance by giving him an opportunity to progress beyond his own primitive mode of thinking through confrontation by concrete data—as when he notes that liquid that looks greater in volume in a tall, thin receptacle is in fact the same as that quantity in a flat, low vessel. Concrete activity that becomes increasingly formal is what leads the child to the kind of mental mobility that approaches the naturally reversible operations of mathematics and logic. The child gradually comes to sense that any change may be mentally cancelled out by the reverse operation—addition by subtraction—or that a change may be counterbalanced by a reciprocal change.

"A child often focuses on only one aspect of a phenomenon at a time, and this interferes with his understanding. We can set up little teaching experiments in such a way that he is forced to pay attention to other aspects. Thus, children up to about age seven estimate the speed of two automobiles by assuming that the one that gets there first is the faster, or that if one passes the other it is faster. To overcome such errors, one can, by using toy automobiles, show that two objects starting at different distances from a finish line cannot be judged by which one arrives first, or show that one car can pass another by circling it and still not finish first. These are simple exercises, but they speed the child toward attending to several features of a situation at once.

"In view of all this it seems highly arbitrary and very likely incorrect to delay the teaching, for example, of Euclidian or metric geometry until the end of the primary grades, particularly when projective geometry has not been given earlier. So too with the teaching of physics, which has much in it that can be profitably taught at an inductive or intuitive level much earlier. Basic notions in these fields are perfectly accessible to children of seven to ten years of age, *provided that they are divorced from their mathematical expression and studied through materials that the child can handle himself.*

"Another matter relates particularly to the ordering of a mathematics curriculum. Often the sequence of psychological development follows more closely the axiomatic order of a subject matter than it does the historical order of development of concepts within the field. One observes, for instance, that certain topological notions, such as connection, separation, being interior to, and so forth, precede the formation of Euclidian and projective notions in geometry, though the former ideas are newer in their formalism in the history of mathematics than the latter. If any special justification were needed for teaching the structure of a subject in its proper logical or axiomatic order rather than its order of historical development, this should provide it. This is not to say that there may not be situations where the historical order is important from the point of view of its cultural or pedagogical relevance.

"As for teaching geometrical notions of perspective and projection, again there is much that can be done by the use of experiments and demonstrations that rest on the child's operational capacity to analyze concrete experience. We have watched children work with an apparatus in which rings of different diameter are placed at different positions between a candle and a screen with a fixed distance between them so that the rings cast shadows of varying sizes on the screen. The child learns how the cast shadow changes size as a function of the distance of the ring from the light source. By bringing to the child such concrete experience of light in revealing situations, we teach him maneuvers that in the end permit him to understand the general ideas underlying projective geometry.

"These examples lead us to think that it is possible to draw up methods of teaching the basic ideas in science and mathematics to children considerably younger than the traditional age. It is at this earlier age that systematic instruction can lay a groundwork in the fundamentals that can be used later and with great profit at the secondary level.

"The teaching of probabilistic reasoning, so very common and important a feature of modern science, is hardly developed in our educational system before college. The omission is probably due to the fact that school syllabi in nearly all countries follow scientific progress with a near-disastrous time lag. But it may also be due to the widespread belief that the understanding of random phenomena depends on the learner's grasp of the meaning of the rarity or commonness of events. And admittedly, such ideas are hard to get across to the young. Our research indicates that the understanding of random phenomena requires, rather, the use of certain concrete logical operations well within the grasp of the young child—provided these operations are free of awkward mathematical expression. Principal among these logical operations are disjunction ('either A *or* B is true') and combination. Games in which lots are drawn, games of roulette, and games involving a gaussian distribution of outcomes are all ideal for giving the child a basic grasp of the logical operation needed for thinking about probability. In such games, children first discover an entirely qualitative notion of chance defined as an uncertain event, contrasted with deductive certainty. The notion of probability as a fraction of certainty is discovered only later. Each of these discoveries can be made before the child ever learns the techniques of the calculus of probabilities or the formal expressions that normally go with probability theory. Interest in problems of a probabilistic nature could easily be awakened and developed before the introduction of any statistical processes or computation. Statistical manipulation and computation are only tools to be used *after* intuitive understanding has been established. If the array of computational paraphernalia is introduced first, then more likely than not it will inhibit or kill the development of probabilistic reasoning.

"One wonders in the light of all this whether it might not be interesting to devote the first two years of school to a series of exercises in manipulating, classifying, and ordering objects in ways that highlight basic operations of logical addition, multiplication, inclusion, serial ordering, and the like. For surely these logical operations are the basis of more specific operations and concepts of all mathematics and science. It may indeed be the case that such an early science and mathematics 'pre-curriculum' might go a long way toward building up in the child the kind of intuitive and more inductive understanding that could be given embodiment later in formal courses in mathematics and science. The effect of such an approach would be, we think, to put more continuity into science and mathematics and also to give the child a much better and firmer comprehension of the concepts which, unless he has this early foundation, he will mouth later without being able to use them in any effective way."

A comparable approach can surely be taken to the teaching of social studies and literature. There has been little research done on the kinds of concepts that a child brings to these subjects, although there is a wealth of observation and anecdote. Can one teach the structure of literary forms by presenting the child with the first part of a story and then having him complete it in the form of a comedy, a tragedy, or a farce—without ever using such words? When, for example, does the idea of "historical trend" develop, and what are its precursors in the child? How does one make a child aware of literary style? Perhaps the child can discover the idea of style through the presentation of the same content written in drastically different styles, in the manner of Beerbohm's *Christmas Garland*. Again, there is no reason to believe that any subject cannot be taught to any child at virtually any age in some form.

Here one is immediately faced with the question of the economy of teaching. One can argue that it might be better to wait until the child is thirteen or fourteen before beginning geometry so that the projective and intuitive first steps can immediately be followed up by a full formal presentation of the subject. Is it worth while to train the young inductively so that they may discover the basic order of knowledge before they can appreciate its formalism? In Professor Inhelder's memorandum, it was suggested that the first two grades might be given over to training the child in the basic logical operations that underlie instruction in mathematics and science. There is evidence to indicate that such rigorous and relevant early training has the effect of making later learning easier. Indeed the experiments on "learning set" seem to indicate just that—that one not only learns specifics but in so doing learns how to learn. So important is training per se that monkeys who have been given extensive training in problem solving suffer considerably less loss and recover more quickly after induced brain damage than animals who had not been previously thus educated. But the danger of such early training may be that it has the effect of training out original but deviant ideas. There is no evidence available on the subject, and much is needed.

The act of learning. Learning a subject seems to involve three almost simultaneous processes. First there is *acquisition* of new information—often information that runs counter to or is a replacement for what the person has previously known implicitly or explicitly. At the very least it is a refinement of previous knowledge. Thus one teaches a student Newton's laws of motion, which violate the testimony of the senses. Or in teaching a student about wave mechanics, one violates the student's belief in mechanical impact as the sole source of real energy transfer. Or one bucks the language and its built-in way of thinking in terms of "wasting energy" by introducing the student to the conservation theorem in physics which asserts that no energy is lost. More often the situation is less drastic, as when one teaches the details of the circulatory system to a student who already knows vaguely or intuitively that blood circulates.

A second aspect of learning may be called *transformation*—the process of manipulating knowledge to make it fit new tasks. We learn to "unmask" or analyze information, to order it in a way that permits extrapolation or interpolation or conversion into another form. Transformation comprises the ways we deal with information in order to go beyond it.

A third aspect of learning is *evaluation:* checking whether the way we have manipulated information is adequate to the task. Is the generalization fitting, have we extrapolated appropriately, are we operating properly? Often a teacher is crucial in helping with evaluation, but much of it takes place by judgments of plausibility without our actually being able to check rigorously whether we are correct in our efforts.

In the learning of any subject matter, there is usually a series of episodes, each episode involving the three processes. Photosynthesis might reasonably comprise material for a learning episode in biology, fitted into a more comprehensive learning experience such as learning about the conversion of energy generally. At its best a learning episode reflects what has gone before it and permits one to generalize beyond it.

A learning episode can be brief or long, contain many ideas or a few. How sustained an episode a learner is willing to undergo depends upon what the person expects to get from his efforts, in the sense of such external things as grades but also in the sense of a gain in understanding.

We usually tailor material to the capacities and needs of students by manipulating learning episodes in several ways: by shortening or lengthening the episode, by piling on extrinsic rewards in the form of praise and gold stars, or by dramatizing the shock of recognition of what the material means when fully understood. The unit in a curriculum is meant to be a recognition of the importance of learning episodes, though many units drag on with no climax in understanding. There is a surprising lack of research on how one most wisely devises adequate learning episodes for children at different ages and in different subject matters. There are many questions that need answers based on careful research, and to some of these we turn now.

There is, to begin with, the question of the balance between extrinsic rewards and intrinsic ones. There has been much written on the role of reward and punishment in learning, but very little indeed on the role of interest and curiosity and the lure of discovery. If it is our intention as teachers to inure the child to longer and longer episodes of learning, it may well be that intrinsic rewards in the form of quickened awareness and understanding will have to be emphasized far more in the detailed design of curricula. One of the least discussed ways of carrying a student through a hard unit of material is to challenge him with a chance to exercise his full powers, so that he may discover the pleasure of full and effective functioning. Good teachers know the power of this lure. Students should know what it feels like to be completely absorbed in a problem. They seldom experience this feeling in school. Given enough absorption in class, some students may be able to carry over the feeling to work done on their own.

There is a range of problems that have to do with how much emphasis should be placed on acquisition, transformation, and evaluation in a learning episode—getting facts, manipulating them, and checking one's ideas. Is it the case, for example, that it is best to give the young child a minimum set of facts first and then encourage him to draw the fullest set of implications possible from this knowledge? In short, should an episode for a young child contain little new information but emphasize what can be done to go beyond that bit on one's own? One teacher of social studies has had great success with fourth-graders through this approach: he begins, for example, with the fact that civilizations have most often begun in fertile river valleys—the only "fact." The students are encouraged in class discussion to figure out why this is the case and why it would be less likely for civilizations to start in mountainous country. The effect of this approach, essentially the technique of discovery, is that the child generates information on his own, which he can then check or evaluate against the sources, getting more new information in the process. This obviously is one kind of learning episode, and doubtless it has limited applicability. What other kinds are there, and are some more appropriate to certain topics and ages than others? It is not the case that "to learn is to learn is to learn," yet in the research literature there appears to be little recognition of differences in learning episodes.

With respect to the optimum length of a learning episode, there are a few commonsense things one can say about it, and these are perhaps interesting enough to suggest fruitful research possibilities. It seems fairly obvious, for example, that the longer and more packed the episode, the greater the pay-off must be in terms of increased power and understanding if the person is to be encouraged to move to a next episode with zest. Where grades are used as a substitute for the reward of understanding, it may well be that learning will cease as soon as grades are no longer given—at graduation.

It also seems reasonable that the more one has a sense of the structure of a subject, the more densely packed and longer a learning episode one can get through without fatigue. Indeed, the amount of new information in any learning episode is really the amount that we cannot quite fit into place at once. And there is a severe limit, as we have already noted, on how much of such un-assimilated information we can keep in mind. The estimate is that adults can handle about seven independent items of information at a time. No norms are available for children—a deplorable lack.

There are many details one can discuss concerning the shaping of learning episodes for children, but the problems that have been mentioned will suffice to give their flavor. Inasmuch as the topic is central to an understanding of how one arranges a curriculum, it seems obvious that here is an area of research that is of the first importance.

The "spiral curriculum." If one respects the ways of thought of the growing child, if one is courteous enough to translate material into his logical forms and challenging enough to tempt him to advance, then it is possible to introduce him at an early age to the ideas and styles that in later life make an educated man. We might ask, as a criterion for any subject taught in primary school, whether, when fully developed, it is worth an adult's knowing, and whether having known it as a child makes a person a better adult. If the answer to both questions is negative or ambiguous, then the material is cluttering the curriculum.

If the hypothesis with which this section was introduced is true—that any subject can be taught to any child in some honest form—then it should follow that a curriculum ought to be built around the great issues, principles, and values that a society deems worthy of the continual concern of its members. Consider two examples—the teaching of literature and of science. If it is granted, for example, that it is desirable to give children an awareness of the meaning of human tragedy and a sense of compassion for it, is it not possible at the earliest appropriate age to teach the literature of tragedy in a manner that illuminates but does not threaten? There are many possible ways to begin: through a re-telling of the great myths, through the use of children's classics, through presentation of and commentary on selected films that have proved themselves. Precisely what kinds of materials should be used at what age with what effect is a subject for research—research of several kinds. We may ask first about the child's conception of the tragic, and here one might proceed in much the same way that Piaget and his colleagues have proceeded in studying the child's conception of physical causality, of morality, of number, and the rest. It is only when we are equipped with such knowledge that we will be in a position to know how the child will translate what-ever we present to him into his own subjective terms. Nor need we wait for all the research findings to be in before proceeding, for a skillful teacher can also experi-ment by attempting to teach what seems to be intuitively right for children of different ages, correcting as he goes. In time, one goes beyond to more complex versions of the same kind of literature or simply revisits some of the same books used earlier. What matters is that later teaching build upon earlier reactions to literature, that it seek to create an ever more explicit and mature under-standing of the literature of tragedy. Any of the great literary forms can be handled in the same way, or any of the great themes—be it the form of comedy or the theme of identity, personal loyalty, or what not.

So too in science. If the understanding of number,

measure, and probability is judged crucial in the pursuit of science, then instruction in these subjects should begin as intellectually honestly and as early as possible in a manner consistent with the child's forms of thought. Let the topics be developed and redeveloped in later grades. Thus, if most children are to take a tenth-grade unit in biology, need they approach the subject cold? Is it not possible, with a minimum of formal laboratory work if necessary, to introduce them to some of the major biological ideas earlier, in a spirit perhaps less exact and more intuitive?

Many curricula are originally planned with a guiding idea much like the one set forth here. But as curricula are actually executed, as they grow and change, they often lose their original form and suffer a relapse into a certain shapelessness. It is not amiss to urge that actual curricula be reexamined with an eye to the issues of continuity and development referred to in the preceding pages. One cannot predict the exact forms that revision might take; indeed, it is plain that there is now available too little research to provide adequate answers. One can only propose that appropriate research be undertaken with the greatest vigor and as soon as possible.

4

INTUITIVE AND ANALYTIC THINKING

Much has been said in the preceding chapters about the importance of a student's intuitive, in contrast to his formal, understanding of the subjects he encounters. The emphasis in much of school learning and student examining is upon explicit formulations, upon the ability of the student to reproduce verbal or numerical formulae. It is not clear, in the absence of research, whether this emphasis is inimical to the later development of good intuitive understanding—indeed, it is even unclear what constitutes intuitive understanding. Yet we can distinguish between inarticulate genius and articulate idiocy—the first represented by the student who, by his operations and conclusions, reveals a deep grasp of a subject but not much ability to "say how it goes," in contrast to the student who is full of seemingly appropriate words but has no matching ability to use the ideas for which the words presumably stand. A careful examination of the nature of intuitive thinking might be of great aid to those charged with curriculum construction and teaching.

Mathematicians, physicists, biologists, and others stress the value of intuitive thinking in their respective areas. In mathematics, for example, intuition is used with two rather different meanings. On the one hand, an individual is said to think intuitively when, having worked for a long time on a problem, he rather suddenly achieves the solution, one for which he has yet to provide a formal proof. On the other hand, an individual is said to be a good intuitive mathematician if, when others come to him with questions, he can make quickly very good guesses whether something is so, or which of several approaches to a problem will prove fruitful.

The development of effectiveness in intuitive thinking is an objective of many of the most highly regarded teachers in mathematics and science. The point has been repeatedly made that in the high school plane geometry is typically taught with excessive emphasis upon techniques, formal proofs, and the like, that much more attention needs to be given to the development of students who have a good intuitive feel for geometry, students who are skillful in discovering proofs, not just in checking the validity of or remembering proofs with which they have been presented. There has been very little done, for example, on the use of diagrams as geometrical experiments as in Hilbert and Cohn's *Geometry and the Imagination*, in which visual proof substitutes for formal proof where possible. Similarly, in physics, Newtonian mechanics is typically taught deductively and analytically. In the judgment of many physicists, at least, there is too little attention to the development of intuitive understanding. Indeed, some have suggested that improving the use of intuitive thinking by teachers is as much a problem as improving its use by students.

Yet, as one member of the Conference put it, it is wrong to look at intuition as "all à la mode and no pie." The good intuiter may have been born with something special, but his effectiveness rests upon a solid knowledge of the subject, a familiarity that gives intuition something to work with. Certainly there are some experiments on learning that indicate the importance of a high degree of mastery of materials in order to operate effectively with them intuitively.

Those concerned with the improvement of curricula in physics and mathematics particularly have often cited as one of their important aims the use of procedures that will contribute to the improvement of intuitive thinking. In their attempts to design such procedures, there has been a question of the kind of systematic psychological knowledge that would be of help. Unfortunately, little systematic knowledge is available about the nature of intuitive thinking or the variables that influence it. What seems most appropriate at this point, therefore, is an attempt to outline the kinds of research which, if even only partially carried out, would begin to provide information useful to those concerned with the improvement of particular courses or, more generally, of the curriculum as a whole. What kinds of questions do we need the answers to?

Questions about the nature of intuitive thinking seem to center upon two large issues: what intuitive thinking is, and what affects it.

One can say many more concrete things about analytic thinking than about intuitive thinking. Analytic thinking characteristically proceeds a step at a time. Steps are explicit and usually can be adequately reported by the thinker to another individual. Such thinking proceeds with relatively full awareness of the information and operations involved. It may involve careful and deductive reasoning, often using mathematics or logic and an explicit plan of attack. Or it may involve a step-by-step process of induction and experiment, utilizing principles of research design and statistical analysis.

In contrast to analytic thinking, intuitive thinking characteristically does not advance in careful, well-defined steps. Indeed, it tends to involve maneuvers based seemingly on an implicit perception of the total problem. The thinker arrives at an answer, which may be right or wrong, with little if any awareness of the process by which he reached it. He rarely can provide an adequate account of how he obtained his answer, and he may be unaware of just what aspects of the problem situation he was responding to. Usually intuitive thinking rests on familiarity with the domain of knowledge involved and with its structure, which makes it possible for the thinker to leap about, skipping steps and employing short cuts in a manner that requires a later rechecking of conclusions by more analytic means, whether deductive or inductive.

The complementary nature of intuitive and analytic thinking should, we think, be recognized. Through intuitive thinking the individual may often arrive at solutions to problems which he would not achieve at all, or at best more slowly, through analytic thinking. Once achieved by intuitive methods, they should if possible be checked by analytic methods, while at the same time being respected as worthy hypotheses for such checking. Indeed, the intuitive thinker may even invent or discover problems that the analyst would not. But it may be the analyst who gives these problems the proper formalism. Unfortunately, the formalism of school learning has somehow devalued intuition. It is the very strong conviction of men who have been designing curricula, in mathematics and the sciences particularly, over the last several years that much more work is needed to discover how we may develop the intuitive gifts of our students from the earliest grades onwards. For, as we have seen, it may be of the first importance to establish an intuitive understanding of materials before we expose our students to more traditional and formal methods of deduction and proof.

As to the nature of intuitive thinking, what is it? It is quite clear that it is not easy either to recognize a particular problem-solving episode as intuitive or, indeed, to identify intuitive ability as such. Precise definition in terms of observable behavior is not readily within our reach at the present time. Obviously, research on the topic cannot be delayed until such a time as a pure and unambiguous definition of intuitive thinking is possible, along with precise techniques for identifying intuition when it occurs. Such refinement is the goal of research, not its starting place. It suffices as a start to ask whether we are able to identify certain problem-solving episodes as more intuitive than others. Or, alternatively, we may ask if we can learn to agree in classifying a person's style or preferred mode of working as characteristically more analytic or inductive, on the one hand, or more intuitive, and, indeed, if we can find some way to classify tasks as ones that require each of those styles of attack. It is certainly clear that it is important not to confuse intuitive and other kinds of thinking with such evaluative notions as effectiveness and ineffectiveness: the analytic, the inductive, and the intuitive can be either. Nor should we distinguish them in terms of whether they produce novel or familiar outcomes, for again this is not the important distinction.

For a working definition of intuition, we do well to begin with Webster: "immediate apprehension or cognition." "Immediate" in this context is contrasted with "mediated"—apprehension or cognition that depends on the intervention of formal methods of analysis and proof. Intuition implies the act of grasping the meaning, significance, or structure of a problem or situation without explicit reliance on the analytic apparatus of one's craft. The rightness or wrongness of an intuition is finally decided not by intuition itself but by the usual methods of proof. It is the intuitive mode, however, that yields hypotheses quickly, that hits on combinations of ideas before their worth is known. In the end, intuition by itself yields a tentative ordering of a body of knowledge that, while it may generate a feeling that the ordering of facts is self-evident, aids principally by giving us a basis for moving ahead in our testing of reality.

Obviously, some intuitive leaps are "good" and some are "bad" in terms of how they turn out. Some men are good intuiters, others should be warned off. What the underlying heuristic of the good intuiter is, is not known but is eminently worthy of study. And what is involved in transforming explicit techniques into implicit ones that can be used almost automatically is a subject that is also full of conjecture. Unquestionably, experience and familiarity with a subject help—but the help is only for some. Those of us who teach graduate students making their first assault on a frontier of knowledge are often struck by our immediate reactions to their ideas, sensing that they are good or impossible or trivial before ever we know why we think so. Often we turn out to be right; sometimes we are victims of too much familiarity with past efforts. In either case, the intuition may be weeks or months ahead of the demonstration of our wisdom or foolhardiness. At the University of Buffalo there is a collection of successive drafts of poems written by leading contemporary poets. One is struck in examining them by the immediate sense one gets of the rightness of a revision a poet has made—but it is often difficult or impossible to say why the revision is better than the original, difficult for the reader and the poet alike.

It is certainly clear that procedures or instruments are needed to characterize and measure intuitive thinking, and that the development of such instruments should be pursued vigorously. We cannot foresee at this stage what the research tools will be in this field. Can one rely, for example, upon the subject's willingness to talk as he works, to reveal the nature of the alternatives he is considering, whether he is proceeding by intuitive leaps or by a step-by-step analysis or by empirical induction? Or will smaller-scale experimental approaches be suitable? Can group measurement procedures involving pencil and paper tests be used to provide a measure? All of these deserve a try.

What variables seem to affect intuitive thinking? There must surely be predisposing factors that are correlated with individual differences in the use of intuition, factors, even, that will predispose a person to think intuitively in one area and not in another. With respect to such factors, we can only raise a series of conjectures. Is the development of intuitive thinking in students more likely if their teachers think intuitively? Perhaps simple imitation is involved, or perhaps more complex processes of identification. It seems unlikely that a student would develop or have confidence in his intuitive methods of thinking if he never saw them used effectively by his elders. The teacher who is willing to guess at answers to questions asked by the class and then subject his guesses to critical analysis may be more apt to build those habits into his students than would a teacher who analyzes everything for the class in advance. Does the providing of varied experience in a particular field increase effectiveness in intuitive thinking in that field? Individuals who have extensive familiarity with a subject appear more often to leap intuitively into a decision or to a solution of a problem—one which later proves to be appropriate. The specialist in internal medicine, for example, may, upon seeing a patient for the first time, ask a few questions, examine the patient briefly, and then make an accurate diagnosis. The risk, of course, is that his method may lead to some big errors as well—bigger than those that result from the more painstaking, step-by-step analysis used by the young intern diagnosing the same case. Perhaps under these circumstances intuition consists in using a limited set of cues, because the thinker knows what things are structurally related to what other things. This is not to say that "clinical" prediction is better or worse than actuarial prediction, only that it is different and that both are useful.

In this connection we may ask whether, in teaching, emphasis upon the structure or connectedness of knowledge increases facility in intuitive thinking. Those concerned with the improvement of the teaching of mathematics often emphasize the importance of developing in the student an understanding of the structure or order of mathematics. The same is true for physics. Implicit in this emphasis, it appears, is the belief that such understanding of structure enables the student, among other things, to increase his effectiveness in dealing intuitively with problems.

What is the effect on intuitive thinking of teaching various so-called heuristic procedures? A heuristic procedure, as we have noted, is in essence a nonrigorous method of achieving solutions of problems. While heuristic procedure often leads to solution, it offers no guarantee of doing so. An algorithm, on the other hand, is a procedure for solving a problem which, if followed accurately, guarantees that in a finite number of steps you will find a solution to the problem if the problem has a solution. Heuristic procedures are often available when no algorithmic procedures are known; this is one of their advantages. Moreover, even when an algorithm is available, heuristic procedures are often much faster. Will the teaching of certain heuristic procedures facilitate intuitive thinking? For example, should students be taught explicitly, "When you cannot see how to proceed with the problem, try to think of a simpler problem that is similar to it; then use the method for solving the simpler problem as a plan for solving the more complicated problem?" Or should the student be led to learn such a technique without actually verbalizing it to himself in that way? It is possible, of course, that the ancient proverb about the caterpillar who could not walk when he tried to say how he did it may apply here. The student who becomes obsessively aware of the heuristic rules he uses to make his intuitive leaps may reduce the process to an analytic one. On the other hand, it is difficult to believe that general heuristic rules —the use of analogy, the appeal to symmetry, the examination of limiting conditions, the visualization of the solution—when they have been used frequently will be anything but a support to intuitive thinking.

Should students be encouraged to guess, in the interest of learning eventually how to make intelligent conjectures? Possibly there are certain kinds of situations where guessing is desirable and where it may facilitate the development of intuitive thinking to some reasonable degree. There may, indeed, be a kind of guessing that requires careful cultivation. Yet, in many classes in school, guessing is heavily penalized and is associated somehow with laziness. Certainly one would not like to educate students to do nothing but guess, for guessing should always be followed up by as much verification and confirmation as necessary; but too stringent a penalty on guessing may restrain thinking of any sort and keep it plodding rather than permitting it to make occasional leaps. May it not be better for students to guess than to be struck dumb when they cannot immediately give the right answer? It is plain that a student should be given some training in recognizing the plausibility of guesses. Very often we are forced, in science and in life generally, to act on the basis of incomplete knowledge; we are forced to guess. According to statistical decision theory, actions based on inadequate data must take account of both probability and costs. What we should teach students to recognize, probably, is when the cost of not guessing is too high, as well as when guessing itself is too costly. We tend to do the latter much better than the former. Should we give our students practice not only in making educated guesses but also in recognizing the characteristics of plausible guesses provided by others—knowing that an answer at least is of the right order of magnitude, or that it is possible rather than impossible? It is our feeling that perhaps a student would be given considerable advantage in his thinking, generally, if he learned that there were alternatives that could be chosen that lay somewhere between truth and complete silence. But let us not confuse ourselves by failing to recognize that there are two kinds of self-confidence— one a trait of personality, and another that comes from knowledge of a subject. It is no particular credit to the educator to help build the first without building the second. The objective of education is not the production of self-confident fools.

Yet it seems likely that effective intuitive thinking is fostered by the development of self-confidence and courage in the student. A person who thinks intuitively may often achieve correct solutions, but he may also be proved wrong when he checks or when others check on him. Such thinking, therefore, requires a willingness to make honest mistakes in the effort to solve problems. One who is insecure, who lacks confidence in himself, may be unwilling to run such risks.

Observations suggest that in business, as the novelty or importance of situations requiring decision increases, the tendency to think analytically also increases. Perhaps when the student sees the consequences of error as too grave and the consequences of success as too chancy, he will freeze into analytic procedures even though they may not be appropriate. On these grounds, one may

65

wonder whether the present system of rewards and punishments as seen by pupils in school actually tends to inhibit the use of intuitive thinking. The assignment of grades in school typically emphasizes the acquisition of factual knowledge, primarily because that is what is most easily evaluated; moreover, it tends to emphasize the correct answer, since it is the correct answer on the straightforward examination that can be graded as "correct." It appears to us important that some research be undertaken to learn what would happen to the development of intuitive thinking if different bases for grading were employed.

Finally, what can be said about the conditions in which intuitive thinking is likely to be particularly effective? In which subjects will mastery be most aided by intuitive procedures followed by checking? Many kinds of problems will be best approached by some combination of intuitive and other procedures, so it is also important to know whether or not both can be developed within the same course by the same teaching methods. This suggests that we examine the mode of effective operation of intuition in different kinds of fields. One hears the most explicit talk about intuition in those fields where the formal apparatus of deduction and induction is most highly developed—in mathematics and physics. The use of the word "intuition" by mathematicians and physicists may reflect their sense of confidence in the power and rigor of their disciplines. Others, however, may use intuition as much or more. Surely the historian, to take but one example, leans heavily upon intuitive procedures in pursuing his subject, for he must select what is relevant. He does not attempt to learn or record everything about a period; he limits himself to finding or learning predictively fruitful facts which, when combined, permit him to make intelligent guesses about what else went on. A comparison of intuitive thinking in different fields of knowledge would, we feel, be highly useful.

We have already noted in passing the intuitive confidence required of the poet and the literary critic in practicing their crafts: the need to proceed in the absence of specific and agreed-upon criteria for the choice of an image of the formulation of a critique. It is difficult for a teacher, a textbook, a demonstration film, to make explicit provision for the cultivation of courage in taste. As likely as not, courageous taste rests upon confidence in one's intuitions about what is moving, what is beautiful, what is tawdry. In a culture such as ours, where there is so much pressure toward uniformity of taste in our mass media of communication, so much fear of idiosyncratic style, indeed a certain suspicion of the idea of style altogether, it becomes the more important to nurture confident intuition in the realm of literature and the arts. Yet one finds a virtual vacuum of research on this topic in educational literature.

The warm praise that scientists lavish on those of their colleagues who earn the label "intuitive" is major evidence that intuition is a valuable commodity in science and one we should endeavor to foster in our students. The case for intuition in the arts and social studies is just as strong. But the pedagogic problems in fostering such a gift are severe and should not be overlooked in our eagerness to take the problem into the laboratory. For one thing, the intuitive method, as we have noted, often produces the wrong answer. It requires a sensitive teacher to distinguish an intuitive mistake—an interestingly wrong leap—from a stupid or ignorant mistake, and it requires a teacher who can give approval and correction simultaneously to the intuitive student. To know a subject so thoroughly that he can go easily beyond the textbook is a great deal to ask of a high school teacher. Indeed, it must happen occasionally that a student is not only more intelligent than his teacher but better informed, and develops intuitive ways of approaching problems that he cannot explain and that the teacher is simply unable to follow or re-create for himself. It is impossible for the teacher properly to reward or correct such students, and it may very well be that it is precisely our more gifted students who suffer such unrewarded effort. So along with any program for developing methods of cultivating and measuring the occurrence of intuitive thinking, there must go some practical consideration of the classroom problems and the limitations on our capacity for encouraging such skills in our students. This, too, is research that should be given all possible support.

These practical difficulties should not discourage psychologists and teachers from making an attack on the problem. Once we have obtained answers to various of the questions raised in this chapter, we shall be in a much better position to recommend procedures for overcoming some of the difficulties.

5

MOTIVES FOR LEARNING

In assessing what might be done to improve the state of the curricular art, we are inevitably drawn into discussion of the nature of motives for learning and the objectives one might expect to attain in educating youth. Obviously, matters of such enormous scope can be considered only briefly here. Yet certain issues seem to be particularly in need of closer scrutiny in relation to the designing of curricula.

In planning a curriculum, one properly distinguishes between the long-run objective one hopes to achieve and certain short-run steps that get one toward that objective. Those of a practical turn of mind are likely to say that little is served by stating long-term objectives unless one can propose short-run methods for their achievement. More idealistic critics may too readily dismiss short-run educational goals on the grounds that they cannot see where they lead. We are inclined to take a middle ground. While one benefits from clarity about the ends of education, it is often true that we may discover or rediscover new ultimate objectives in the process of trying to reach more modest goals. Something of this order seems to have occurred in recent efforts to improve school curricula.

The efforts of the past decade began with the modest intention of doing a better job of teaching physics or mathematics or some other subject. The impulse that led a group of highly competent physicists, for example, to join together in this effort was the sense of how great a gap had developed between physics as known by the physicist and physics as taught in school, a gap of particular importance because of revolutionary advances in science and the crisis in national security. But as the effort broadened, as scholars and scientists from other disciplines entered the field, a broader objective began to emerge. It is clear that there is in American education today a new emphasis upon the pursuit of excellence. There appear to be several things implied by the pursuit of excellence that have relevance not only to what we teach, but to how we teach and how we arouse the interest of our students.

The view has already been expressed that the pursuit of excellence must not be limited to the gifted student. But the idea that teaching should be aimed at the average student in order to provide something for everybody is an equally inadequate formula. The quest, it seems to many of us, is to devise materials that will challenge the superior student while not destroying the confidence and will-to-learn of those who are less fortunate. We have no illusions about the difficulty of such a course, yet it is the only one open to us if we are to pursue excellence and at the same time honor the diversity of talents we must educate. Much has already been said about the importance of preparing curricula adequate to this end, of educating teachers, of using all available teaching aids. These are steps toward the achievement of excellence. Another essential step has to do with motivation.

Arnold Bennett remarked that the French sacrifice the girl to the woman; the English, the woman to the girl. How do we fare? It has been said of the American high school that its emphasis on the "peer" culture negates some of the adult aims of education. The claim is debatable, but the issue is a real one, as such commentators on the social setting of American secondary education as James Coleman and David Riesman have pointed out. One need only examine the advertisements directed to the teen-age set to sense the central role of social life and "the sociables." Studies of American high-school culture point particularly to the higher value placed on social popularity than upon academic achievement. Yet the 1960 *Report on Admissions Policy* prepared by a Committee of the Harvard Faculty under the chairmanship of Professor Franklin Ford indicates that Harvard students enrolled from public high schools carry away more honors than students of like aptitude enrolled from the great independent preparatory schools of the Eastern seaboard. It may well be that the high school students in the Harvard group are the outstanding ones in their schools, but, even at that, it would certainly indicate that at the very least American high schools are not ruining these students for later outstanding work.

Granting, then, that the situation is not as black as some would have us believe nor yet as good as some would like to hope, what can be said about motives for learning in our schools? What results from emphasis upon units of curriculum, upon grades and promotion, upon rote examinations, and the rest, with respect to the continuity and deepening of school learning?

71

Somewhere between apathy and wild excitement, there is an optimum level of aroused attention that is ideal for classroom activity. What is that level? Frenzied activity fostered by the competitive project may leave no pause for reflection, for evaluation, for generalization, while excessive orderliness, with each student waiting passively for his turn, produces boredom and ultimate apathy. There is a day-to-day problem here of great significance. Short-run arousal of interest is not the same as the long-term establishment of interest in the broader sense. Films, audio-visual aids, and other such devices may have the short-run effect of catching attention. In the long run, they may produce a passive person waiting for some sort of curtain to go up to arouse him. We do not know. Perhaps anything that holds the child's attention is justified on the ground that eventually the child will develop a taste for more self-controlled attention— a point on which there is no evidence. The issue is particularly relevant in an entertainment-oriented, mass-communication culture where passivity and "spectatorship" are dangers. Perhaps it is in the technique of arousing attention in school that first steps can be taken to establish that active autonomy of attention that is the antithesis of the spectator's passivity.

There will always be, perhaps, mixed motives for learning among schoolchildren. There are parents and teachers to be pleased, one's contemporaries to be dealt with, one's sense of mastery to be developed. At the same time, interests are developing, the world opens up. Schoolwork is only a part of the quickened life of the growing child. To different children it means different things. To some it is the road to parental approbation;

72

to others it is an intrusion on the social world of contemporaries, and is to be handled by the minimum effort that will "get by." The culture of the school may be anti-intellectual or quite the opposite. And within this complex picture there is the subtle attraction of the subjects in school that a child finds interesting. One can spell out the details of the picture, but in the main they are familiar enough. How, within this context, do we arouse the child's interest in the world of ideas?

Several tentative recommendations have already been made in the spirit of suggesting needed research. Principal among these were increasing the inherent interest of materials taught, giving the student a sense of discovery, translating what we have to say into the thought forms appropriate to the child, and so on. What this amounts to is developing in the child an interest in what he is learning, and with it an appropriate set of attitudes and values about intellectual activity generally. Surely we shall not by presently conceivable reforms create a nation of devoted intellectuals, nor is it apparent that this should be the major guiding aim of our schools. Rather, if teaching is done well and what we teach is worth learning, there are forces at work in our contemporary society that will provide the external prod that will get children more involved in the process of learning than they have been in the past.

Our cultural climate has not been marked traditionally by a deep appreciation of intellectual values. We have as a people always expressed a great faith in education. There are many reasons for this—the absence of an aristocracy, the pragmatic demands inherent in a frontier society, and so on—but these need not concern us here.

Education has been conceived as a means to better the lot of our children rather than our own lot; it is almost a universal belief that children should have a better educational opportunity than their parents. Yet for all our reverence for education, we have paid little enough attention to its content: a vague reference to the "three R's" has seemed sufficient. We have been a country in which doing has been taken as the mark of effectiveness in thinking, and, perhaps more than any other major Western power, we have conceived of the gap between theory and practice as a yawning one. Insofar as we have idealized the thinker, it has been in the form of celebrating arcane wizardry as in the case of Einstein, who was presumably incomprehensible but brilliant, or of rewarding the practical accomplishments that have followed from thought. Thomas Edison was our conception of the American scientist as engineer. The writer, the poet, the theorist, and the savant have not been folk figures in America, have not stimulated legends.

Today, many Americans have become conscious, not just of the practical virtues of education, but of its content and quality—what it is and what it might be. Several factors are contributing to this trend. We are moving into a new era of scientific technology, a second industrial revolution, perhaps more drastic than the first one of over a century ago. Control systems, automation, new sources of power, new space to explore— all of these have livened interest in the nature of our schools and what our young people are learning in them. Unquestionably, there has also been a surge of awareness born of our sense of imperiled national security.

The Soviet Union's conquests in space, its capability of producing not only powerful weapons but also an effective industrial society, have shaken American complacency to a degree that, looking back, would have seemed inconceivable a decade ago. And, finally, part of the growing interest in education comes from the fact that the American population now contains a very high proportion of college graduates. We also have the good fortune to be wealthy. The proportion of young people graduating from college today is higher than the proportion graduating from high school forty years ago. All of these factors have stimulated a renewal of interest in education that is making itself felt among students and parents alike.

There is much discussion about how to give our schools a more serious intellectual tone, about the relative emphasis on athletics, popularity, and social life on the one hand and on scholarly application on the other. There is an effort afoot throughout the nation to redress what has clearly been an imbalance. Admiration for and interest in scholarship is likely to increase faster than expected. There are even some amusing sidelights in which the old symbols are being poured into new bottles—as in certain high schools where the coveted athlete's "letter" is being given as well to students who make distinguished grade averages. But there is another problem, more remote in time, that may eventually prove more serious and for which planning can now be effectively undertaken.

It is highly probable that certain changes in our educational system will occur in the years ahead, given the demands placed upon it by the community. The first is that there will be an increasing demand for the teaching

75

of science, technology, and supporting subjects. Jobs will be abundant in the newer technical industries. The decentralized American school system has always responded to the opportunities available in American industry and will respond again. It is very difficult to tell on the basis of population statistics and of extrapolations of economic developments when the supply and demand for such technical specialists will meet. At the present time we are far from it. Some estimates suggest that within twenty years, as a combined result of the increased training of engineers and the postwar baby crop now reaching college age, the first part of this demand will be taken up. What will occur after that will depend upon a host of factors, not the least of which will be the speed and thoroughness with which American industry absorbs the new scientific technology available to it.

A second almost inevitable consequence of the national security crisis is that there will be a quickened flow of federal funds in support of education at the state and local levels. The present National Defense Education Act is only a beginning. A likely, though scarcely inevitable, consequence of federal aid is that there may be a reduction in the disparity in quality that now exists among local school systems. The lower limit of teachers' salaries is likely to increase faster than the upper limit, and better school facilities everywhere will be available as a result of present and proposed legislation on school construction.

Both of these trends—increasing emphasis on technological progress and federal aid in the interest of coping with the competitive crisis that America must face as a world power—are likely to lead to one result that has questionable consequences for American education and American life unless change is planned well in advance. Let us not be so involved in present efforts to improve the intellectual level of American schools that we overlook preparations for dealing with our success in doing so. The peril of success under the conditions sketched is the growth of what has been called "meritocracy." Partly out of the inertia of present practice and partly in response to the challenge of the new developments described earlier, there will be a strong tendency to move the able student ahead faster and particularly to move him ahead if he shows early promise in technical or scientific fields. Planned carefully, such acceleration can be good for the student and for the nation. A meritocracy, however, implies a system of competition in which students are moved ahead and given further opportunities on the basis of their achievement, with position in later life increasingly and irreversibly determined by earlier school records. Not only later educational opportunities but subsequent job opportunities become increasingly fixed by earlier school performance. The late bloomer, the early rebel, the child from an educationally indifferent home—all of them, in a full-scale meritocracy, become victims of an often senseless irreversibility of decision.

A meritocracy is likely to have several undesirable effects on the climate in which education occurs, though with advance planning we may be able to control them. One consequence may be an overemphasis upon examination performance. C. P. Snow's Rede Lecture of 1959 (*The Two Cultures and the Scientific Revolutions*, Cambridge, 1959) contains these comments (pp. 19–20) on the Cambridge Mathematical Tripos. They might well give us pause: "For over a hundred years, the nature of the Tripos had been crystallizing. The Competition for the top places had got fiercer, and careers hung on them. In most colleges, certainly in my own, if one managed to come out as a Senior or Second Wrangler, one was elected a Fellow out of hand. A whole apparatus of coaching had grown up. Men of the quality of Hardy, Littlewood, Russell, Eddington, Jeans, Keynes, went in for two or three years' training for an examination that was intensely competitive and intensely difficult. Most people in Cambridge were very proud of it, with a similar pride to that which almost anyone in England always has for our existing educational institutions, whatever they happen to be. . . . In every respect but one, the old Mathematical Tripos seemed perfect. The one exception, however, appeared to some to be rather important. It was simply—so the young creative mathematicians, such as Hardy and Littlewood, kept saying—that the training had no intellectual merit at all. They went a little further, and said that the Tripos had killed serious mathematics in England stone dead for a hundred years." It is, to be sure, highly unlikely that anything approaching the fierceness of the Mathematical Tripos would develop in the United States, and certainly not at the level of our high schools and primary schools. But caricatured extremes help quicken understanding. If it should become the case that certain highly desirable jobs are assured to winners of National Merit Scholarships, then we may be quite sure that it will not be long before teaching and learning reflect the importance of such scholarships. If, further, the principal scholarships and prizes come increasingly to be awarded for merit in the sciences and mathematics, then we may also expect, and this is another danger we face, that there will be a devaluation of other forms of scholarly enterprise. Literature, history, and the arts will, under such circumstances, likely become the prerogative of a group whose family values rather than school values provide the principal support for the pursuit of these topics. Good teachers in the nonscientific subjects will be harder to recruit, harder to attract into teaching. Motives for learning in these fields will become feebler. One exaggerates, to be sure, but these are all possible contingencies that should be guarded against.

Perhaps it would not be amiss at this point in our educational history to consider the forms of countervailing activity that might prevent such an eventual outcome. We can ill afford an alienated group of literary intellectuals who feel that advances in science, which they may fail to understand out of a sense of being shunned by the system of rewards for technical and scientific achievement, betoken the destruction of traditional culture. It is certainly plain that at the very least there will have to be energy devoted to improving curricula and teaching in the humanities and social sciences comparable to what is now being devoted to science and mathematics. Future legislative provisions for federal and state aid to education might well include specific titles concerned with such problems, and it is none too early to consider, before appropriate legislative committees, the nature and extent of such support.

Emphasis on competitive performance in the scientific subjects can, of course, be converted to useful ends through imaginativeness and flexibility in the construction of examinations. An examination can also foster thoughtfulness. Special counseling will be necessary in what is almost certain to be a more competitive school system than we ever have known before in America. It will be needed not only for the student who is moving ahead rapidly but more especially for the student—and he represents an important segment of our younger population—who is not the fast, early, and steady producer.

But remedies such as better examinations and counseling do not provide the major answer. If the dangers of meritocracy and competitiveness, the risks of an overemphasis on science and technology, and the devaluation of humanistic learning are to be dealt with, we shall have to maintain and nurture a vigorous pluralism in America. The theatre, the arts, music, and the humanities as presented in our schools and colleges will need the fullest support.

To sum up the matter, motives for learning must be kept from going passive in an age of spectatorship, they must be based as much as possible upon the arousal of interest in what there is to be learned, and they must be kept broad and diverse in expression. The danger signs of meritocracy and a new form of competitiveness are already in evidence. Already it is possible to see where advance planning can help. Such planning and the research to support it should be given high priority.

6

AIDS TO TEACHING

THERE has been a great deal of discussion in recent years about the devices that can be employed to aid in the teaching process. These devices are of many kinds. Some of them are designed to present material to the student of a kind that would not be available to him in his ordinary school experience. Films, TV, microphotographic film, film strips, sound recordings, and the like are among the devices ordinarily employed in such work. Books also serve in this role. These are the tools by which the student is given vicarious though "direct" experience of events. It does not serve much to dismiss such materials as "merely for enrichment," since it is obvious that such enrichment is one of the principal objectives of education. Let us call these *devices for vicarious experience.*

A second type of teaching aid has the function of helping the student to grasp the underlying structure of a phenomenon—to sense the genotype behind the phenotype, to use terms from genetics. The well wrought laboratory experiment or demonstration is the classic aid in such activity. A closer look at our efforts to get students to grasp structure indicates that there are many other devices and exercises that have the same function. The effort to give visible embodiment to ideas in mathematics is of the same order as the laboratory work. The

Stern blocks, Cuisenaire rods, and Dienes blocks, as well as the demonstrations of Piaget and Inhelder mentioned earlier, have the same function. So too do certain kinds of charts and representations, either in animated or still form. Models, such as a model of the molecule or an idealized model of the respiratory system, serve a comparable function. Needless to say, films and television as well as adroitly illustrated books can be adjuncts to the effort at producing clarity and concrete embodiment.

But there are other, more subtle devices that can be and are being used to lead the student to a sense of the conceptual structure of things he observes. Perhaps the best way to characterize them is to call them "sequential programs." There are certain orders of presentation of materials and ideas in any subject that are more likely than others to lead the student to the main idea. The courses being devised by the University of Illinois Committee on School Mathematics, the School Mathematics Study Group, the Physical Science Study Committee, and others are excellent instances of the well conceived sequence designed to lead the student to an understanding of basic ideas and structures.

The whole range of aids from the laboratory exercise through the mathematical blocks to the programmed sequence we shall, for convenience, speak of as *model devices*.

Closely related to these are what might be called *dramatizing devices*. The historical novel that is true in spirit to its subject, the nature film that dramatizes the struggle of a species in its habitat, the exemplification of an experiment executed by a dramatic personality, exposure to greatness in government by a documentary on the life and service of a Winston Churchill—all these can have the dramatic effect of leading the student to identify more closely with a phenomenon or an idea. Undoubtedly, this "aid" in teaching can best be exemplified by the drama-creating personality of a teacher. But there are many additional dramatic aids upon which teachers can and do call—and one wonders whether they are called upon often enough.

Finally, the past decade has witnessed the emergence of various *automatizing devices*, teaching machines, to aid in teaching. While such devices vary quite widely, they have certain features in common. The machine presents a carefully programmed order of problems or exercises to the student, one step at a time. The student responds selectively in one form or another to the alternatives presented in a problem or exercise. The machine then responds immediately, indicating whether the response was or was not correct. If a correct response is made, the machine moves to the next problem. The progression in difficulty from problem to problem is usually quite gradual in order to keep the student from the discouragement of excessive failure.

What one teaches and how one teaches it with the aid of such devices depends upon the skill and wisdom that goes into the construction of a program of problems. The art of programming a machine is, of course, an extension of the art of teaching. To date, most of the programming has been intuitive and has been entrusted to a teacher of known reputation. It has been remarked by teachers who have written tapes for teaching machines that the exercise has the effect of making one highly conscious of the sequence in which one presents problems and of the aims of the sequence—whether, for example, one is trying to get children to memorize material or use material cumulatively in doing progressively more difficult problems.

Perhaps the technically most interesting features of such automatic devices are that they can take some of the load of teaching off the teacher's shoulders, and, perhaps more important, that the machine can provide immediate correction or feedback to the student while he is in the act of learning. It is still far too early to evaluate the eventual use of such devices, and it is highly unfortunate that there have been such exaggerated claims made by both proponents and opponents. Clearly, the machine is not going to replace the teacher—indeed, it may create a demand for more and better teachers if the more onerous part of teaching can be relegated to automatic devices. Nor does it seem likely that machines will have the effect of dehumanizing learning any more than books dehumanize learning. A program for a teaching machine is as personal as a book: it can be laced with humor or be grimly dull, can either be a playful activity or be tediously like a close-order drill.

In sum, then, there exist devices to aid the teacher in extending the student's range of experience, in helping him to understand the underlying structure of the material he is learning, and in dramatizing the significance of what he is learning. There are also devices now being developed that can take some of the load of teaching from the teacher's shoulders. How these aids and devices should be used in concert as a system of aids is, of course, the interesting problem.

The matter of "integration" is nicely illustrated in a report on the teaching films used by the Physical Science

Study Committee. "Until quite recently, most educational films were enrichment films, designed primarily to introduce phenomena or experiences that would otherwise be unavailable inside the classroom. Such films are necessarily self-contained, since the producer is ignorant of what his audience has previously learned or what it will go on to learn; he can neither build upon the student's immediate past nor lay the groundwork for his immediate future. In the last few years, another kind of educational film, stimulated to a large extent by television, has made its appearance. These films present the entire substance of a course, and are designed to minimize the need for a teacher. Clearly, it is possible to make extremely useful films in either of these forms, and such films have indeed been made." Stephen White, who has had a major part in producing the films used in the high school physics course prepared by the PSSC, then goes on to say in his report on the film work of that group, "Every film produced by the PSSC must meet two conditions. It must (1) further the presentation of the PSSC course as a whole, and (2) set the tone and level of the course. For the PSSC film is part of a complex that includes also the text, the laboratory, the classroom, the student, and the teacher."

White describes some of the problems of making the film fit. "The film must fit into this complex and never disrupt it. Obviously, this principle imposes serious restrictions on the producer. The most important of these for the PSSC films lies in the relation between the film and the laboratory. Only at his peril may the producer include in a film experiments which the student should and could do in the laboratory. Occasionally such an

85

experiment will be included because it is essential to the logical development of the film's theme, in which case it is done briefly and allusively. More often, it is considered desirable to repeat on film, with more sophisticated apparatus, an experiment that is suitable for the school laboratory; in such cases the film is made in a manner which indicates clearly that it should be shown *after* the student has done the lab work, and the teacher is strongly urged to defer it until that time."

Other elements in the complex must also be taken into account. "Other restrictions on the film require it to follow the logical development, the spirit, and the vocabulary (where it exists) of the text. Finally, the film must always respect the position of the teacher; it must leave for him those activities which are necessary for him if he is to retain the respect of his class. All these are negative, but the film makes positive contributions to the complex as well. It serves the classroom by directing attention to those aspects of the subject which will best stimulate classroom discussion. Thus, the PSSC film on Work and Mechanical Energy' deliberately calls attention to the temperature rise in a nail on which work is being done, and thus opens discussion of thermal energy, which the class will meet next. And the film, wherever possible, serves the individual student directly by suggesting work he himself can carry on outside the school; it is for this reason that many PSSC films contain sophisticated experiments performed with simple apparatus."

The writer discusses a second function performed by the integrated teaching film: "The second condition that every film must meet—that of setting level and tone—may well be the most important contribution that the film medium can make. By directing attention to the important questions and the important problems, the film can help assure that all the great mass of fact and concept and theory and application that constitute any field of knowledge will fall into a coherent pattern in which the more important aspects will be clearly differentiated from the trivial. This is most difficult to achieve with the printed word; on film it can be accomplished at times with a gesture. Beyond meeting these two conditions, PSSC attempts in each film to make other substantial contributions to the learning process. Each film shows a real scientist in action, presenting him not as a disembodied intellect but as a normal, active, occasionally fallible human being, dealing rigorously and respectfully with real problems and deriving not only satisfaction but at times excitement from the intellectual pursuit in which he is engaged. It is in this implicit fashion that the films attempt to elucidate the nature of scientists and of the scientific life. . . . The films are scrupulously honest. Experiments that are seen on the screen were carefully performed and are accurately reported. The temptation to use the legerdemain inherent in film processes has been steadily resisted, and in those rare cases where it is used to produce a desirable effect, the student is told explicitly how it is used and why."

The task of the PSSC—the creation of a single high school course in physics—was a specialized one, and the particular problems of the course may not relate to all forms of curriculum construction. Yet there is always a question as to the purpose of any particular device—be it a film of paramecia or a slide projection of a graph or a television show on the Hoover Dam. *The devices them-*

selves cannot dictate their purpose. Unbridled enthusiasm for audio-visual aids or for teaching machines as panaceas overlooks the paramount importance of what one is trying to accomplish. A perpetual feast of the best teaching films in the world, unrelated to other techniques of teaching, could produce bench-bound passivity. Limiting instruction to a steady diet of classroom recitation supported only by traditional and middling textbooks can make lively subjects dull for the student. The objectives of a curriculum and the balanced means for attaining it should be the guide.

A discussion of teaching aids may seem like an unusual context in which to consider the teacher's role in teaching. Yet, withal, the teacher constitutes the principal aid in the teaching process as it is practiced in our schools. What can be said of the teacher's role in teaching?

It takes no elaborate research to know that communicating knowledge depends in enormous measure upon one's mastery of the knowledge to be communicated. That much is obvious enough—whether the teacher uses other aids or not. It is also quite plain from recent surveys that many primary and secondary school teachers are not, in the view of various official bodies, sufficiently well trained initially to teach their subject. It is also the case that, with the present high turnover in the teaching profession, even relatively well prepared teachers do not have sufficient opportunity to learn their subjects in that special way that comes from teaching it. For teaching is a superb way of learning. There is a beautiful story about a distinguished college teacher of physics. He reports introducing an advanced class to the quantum theory: "I went through it once and looked up only to find the class full of blank faces—they had obviously not understood. I went through it a second time and they still did not understand it. And so I went through it a third time, and that time *I* understood it."

There are certain measures that must be taken to improve the quality of teachers, steps that have been proposed many times and that need no elaboration here. Better recruitment and the possibility of better selection, better substantive education in teacher training institutions, on-the-job training of younger teachers by more experienced ones, in-service and summer institutes, closed-circuit television to continue the education of teachers, improvement in teachers' salaries—all of these must obviously be pursued as objectives. But equally important is the upgrading of the prestige of the teaching profession. This upgrading will depend upon the degree to which we in America are serious about educational reform and the degree to which efforts are made to improve not only the facilities and salaries available to teachers but the support they can count on from the community and from our universities.

One special matter concerning the teacher as communicator of knowledge must be mentioned: the training and qualifications of the elementary-school teachers. Several references have already been made to the training of children concretely and intuitively in logical operations that will later be taught more formally in upper primary and secondary school. Such teaching requires special training, and it is not clear what the most effective form of training is. Special emphasis should very likely be given to such work—research on how to train teachers for such teaching along with research on the actual teaching of younger pupils.

The teacher is not only a communicator but a model. Somebody who does not see anything beautiful or powerful about mathematics is not likely to ignite others with a sense of the intrinsic excitement of the subject. A teacher who will not or cannot give play to his own intuitiveness is not likely to be effective in encouraging intuition in his students. To be so insecure that he dares not be caught in a mistake does not make a teacher a likely model of daring. If the teacher will not risk a shaky hypothesis, why should the student?

To communicate knowledge and to provide a model of competence, the teacher must be free to teach and to learn. We have not been sufficiently mindful of the ways in which such freedom can be achieved. Notably, we have been neglectful of the uses to which educated parents can be put. Various schools have experimented successfully with plans that use parents for the semi-professional tasks that keep teachers pinned down. Parents can certainly help in supervising study halls, in grading routine quizzes, in preparing laboratory materials, and in the dozens of routine operations necessary in a school. The effect would be to free the teacher for teaching and study. If the teacher is also learning, teaching takes on a new quality.

The teacher is also an immediately personal symbol of the educational process, a figure with whom students can identify and compare themselves. Who is not able to recall the impact of some particular teacher—an enthusiast, a devotee of a point of view, a disciplinarian whose ardor came from love of a subject, a playful but serious mind? There are many images, and they are precious. Alas, there are also destructive images: the teachers who sapped confidence, the dream killers, and the rest of the cabinet of horrors.

Whitehead once remarked that education should involve an exposure to greatness. Many of us have been fortunate. But there is no simple plan for attracting greatness to the teaching profession. Emphasis on excellence is still the slow but likely way. Might it not be the case, however, that television and film might expand the range of identification figures—models of greatness—within the special limits imposed by one-way communication? We know relatively little about effective identification figures for children at different ages and in different circumstances. Are Olympian models the only ones or the best ones for engaging a child's sense of competence or greatness? Perhaps promising high school students as guest teachers from time to time would do better? They might also lure more talent into teaching.

In sum, then, the teacher's task as communicator, model, and identification figure can be supported by a wise use of a variety of devices that expand experience, clarify it, and give it personal significance. There need be no conflict between the teacher and the aids to teaching. There will be no conflict if the development of aids takes into account the aims and the requirements of teaching. The film or television show as gimmick, the television system without substance or style in its programs, the pictographically vivid portrayal of the trivial—these will help neither the teacher nor the student. Problems of quality in a curriculum cannot be dodged by the purchase of sixteen-millimeter projection equipment. The National Defense Education Act provides considerable sums of money for the development of audio-visual aids. The intelligent use of that money and of other resources now available will depend upon how well we are able to integrate the technique of the film maker or the program producer with the technique and wisdom of the skillful teacher.

INDEX

INDEX

Accelerated studies, 77

Accuracy, 39

Aids to teaching, 81–92; balanced use of, 84, 88, 92; relation of teacher to, 15f, 84, 86, 88, 91; categories of devices, 81–83; teaching machines, 15, 83f; audio-visual aids, 15, 20, 72, 92; NDEA provisions, 92

Algorithm, 63

Alpert, Richard, xii

American Association for the Advancement of Science, ix

Analytic thinking, 57f, 59f

Audio-visual aids, see Aids to teaching

Automatizing devices, 83

Beard, Charles A., 3

Bennett, Arnold, 71

Biological Sciences Curriculum Study, 2, 19

Cambridge Mathematical Tripos, 77f

Carnegie Corporation of New York, ix

Citizenship training, 9

Cognitive operations: preoperational thought, 34f, 41–43; concrete operations, 35–37, 38, 42f; formal operations, 37

Cohn-Vossen, Stephan, 56

Coleman, James, 71

Commager, Henry Steele, 3

Commission on Mathematics, 2

Comprehensive high school, 5

Conant, James Bryant, 5

Counseling, 80

Cronbach, Lee, xiv

Cuisenaire rods, 82

Curriculum design, 1, 18, 54; long-range objectives vs. short-term goals, 69f; social factors in, 8f

Curriculum lag, 26, 45, 70

Development, see Intellectual development

Dienes blocks, 82

Discovery, role of, 20-22

"Doing" vs. "understanding," 29f

Dramatizing devices, 82f

Educational Testing Service, 31

Enriched curriculum, 11, 81

Examinations, 30f, 55, 71, 79f

Excellence, pursuit of, 9, 70

Exemplifications of principles: tropisms, 6f; algebra, 7f; language, 8; social geography, 21f, 50f; tides, 22f; Triangular Trade, 23f; *Moby Dick*, 24; gravitation, 24; *Lord Jim*, 24; Hundred Years' War, 25; concept of function, 28f; pinball, 35f; conservation theorem, 41f; projective geometry, 44; *Christmas Garland*, 47

Federal aid to education, ix, 76, 79; National Defense Education Act, 76, 92

Finlay, Gilbert, xiv

Ford, Franklin L., 71

Franklin, Benjamin, 4

Friedman, Francis L., xii

General science, 26f, 44f, 46